PEOPLE, TECHNOLOGY, PROFIT:
PRACTICAL IDEAS FOR A HAPPIER, HEALTHIER PRACTICE BUSINESS

1ST Edition

LAURIE MORGAN, MBA

The Management Rx Collection

Management Rx

San Francisco, CA

People, Technology, Profit:
Practical Ideas for a Happier, Healthier Practice Business

Cover photos, from left to right:
© JohnKwan - Fotolia.com
© Andres Rodriguez–Fotolia.com
© ArtemSam – Fotolia.com
© Monkey Business Images – iStockphoto.com

ISBN-13: 978-0692816516 (Management Rx)
First print edition published December, 2016.

Table of Contents

Introducing ... the Capko & Morgan book club!

Capko & Morgan's new book club for readers of Laurie Morgan's *People, Technology, Profit* and Judy Capko's *Secrets of the Best-Run Practices* will launch in early 2017.

This new club will feature special offers on upcoming releases from Laurie and Judy, plus exclusive, members-only events and other benefits. And just by holding this book in your hand, you're eligible to join—for free.

To learn more, email Laurie and Judy at info@capko.com

Foreword

People, Technology, Profit: Practical Ideas for a Happier, Healthier Practice Business sets high expectations, but delivers on them for physicians, health care executives, and office managers. Laurie Morgan understands the essential inner workings of a medical practice business. Using her intuition, education, and experience, she brings you practical solutions to critical administrative problems facing medical practices of every size and most specialties.

Physicians are challenged to have the best technical skills. They invest years in medical education at the country's best universities and internship and residency, followed by years' more within their specialty in fellowships, in hospitals, and in practice. But this training omits the knowledge that is essential to running a busy medical practice. Physician-owners are expected to excel in business operations, human resource management, and finances with no training—while also being charming with their patients, understanding even their unspoken needs and wants. This book discusses key business functions where problems often emerge requiring attention and expertise to solve. You will discover how a skilled consultant pinpoints the source of problems—a source that is often overlooked or misunderstood by the practice team. You will likely be surprised by some of Laurie's non-traditional recommendations, but she will help you understand the rationale behind these insightful ideas.

Through her vivid case studies, she walks the reader through problems with solutions that don't break the bank, but rather afford you the opportunity to become more profitable.

It begins with your people, understanding and appreciating their role in a happier, more profitable practice. Laurie points out that although staff is usually one of a practice's largest expenses, squeezing staff costs can compromise your ability to generate more revenue, and cause service to decline. If you staff well, respecting and using employees' talents wisely, they will improve service and contribute to the bottom line, not erode it.

You will gain a front row view of the immense technology opportunities that exist, with insight about innovations that address the multiple, changing demands of medical practice. Laurie will help you understand the enormous gains you can make in efficiency, service, and profits by investing in new technology, using specific improvements her clients have made as examples. Readers that haven't yet embraced technology will want to explore new tools that can help with everything from smoother workflow to better financial performance—while also achieving customer service gains and the increased employee satisfaction that comes from opportunity for growth. Laurie even discusses how technology has changed the way medical practices market, and how you can do it economically. You will quickly become a fan of technology once you understand the benefits.

I have the utmost respect for Laurie and her many professional accomplishments. She is a natural writer and does it with authority and confidence. Her writing is fluid and easy to understand, even when she describes the most complex situations. She is also a brilliant consultant who cares deeply about her clients and their future. She knows how hard doctors work, she knows how committed and talented so many administrators and managers are, and she also cares about the staff—understanding how much they contribute to a practice's success. There is a lot of brainpower in your practice and here's your chance to tap into it. Laurie is smart and you will be smarter after you read *People, Technology, Profit*.

—*Judy Capko, Thousand Oaks, CA, 11/30/2016*

Acknowledgements

This book might never have happened without the support of my Capko & Morgan partners. They are always up for brainstorming, full of good ideas, and able to make even the most laborious projects fun. I am so lucky to work with you every day, Judy Capko and Joe Capko, and so grateful for your help with the book.

About the Author

Laurie Morgan is medical practice management consultant, author, and presenter. Her consulting work focuses on revenue, operating efficiency, staffing strategies, technology, and marketing. She has written articles on these subjects for a wide range of medical publications and websites.

In 2013, Laurie founded her publishing line, <u>Management Rx</u>. Today the series includes eight individual ebooks as well as *People, Technology, Profit: Practical Ideas for a Happier, Healthier Practice Business.*

Laurie's work with medical practices draws on her 20 years' experience in management, which has included senior management roles in both large corporate settings and startups. Laurie has an MBA from Stanford University and an AB in Economics from Brown University.

Introduction

What management strategies, tools, and techniques can best help medical practices not just survive, but thrive? This is the unifying question that ties together the stories and ideas in this book, and, not coincidentally, guides my consulting work.

When Joe Capko encouraged me to join Capko & Company back in 2009, I was intrigued. Medical practices face unique management challenges, especially in handling third party payments and regulatory requirements. But beyond the intellectual appeal, it seemed to me that practice management consulting offered an opportunity to contribute, at least in a small way, to improving healthcare. At some point, we will all rely on the help of a skilled doctor. Stronger medical practice businesses—enterprises in which physicians feel valued and can thrive—ultimately benefit us all.

Trends that favor large organizations and physician employment tend to dominate the healthcare media headlines. But other factors that get less attention favor smaller, more flexible, independent practice structures. That tension is healthy. Maintaining options is a good thing for physicians and patients alike. Some physicians and patients will always prefer larger organizations, others will prefer a more personal or entrepreneurial experience. To continue to attract the motivated, highly intelligent people that medicine requires, physician careers must continue to offer choices, too.

In recent years, technologies and ideas have emerged that can make the business side of medical practice easier to manage—for practices of all shapes and sizes. Innovation in technology and management offers the possibility of not just maintaining practice options for physicians and patients, but even expanding them. I love working with physicians, healthcare executives, and practice managers to implement new solutions to make their businesses run better, whatever form those businesses take.

This book features case studies and ideas drawn from my work with real practice clients. Each "part" of this book is based on material previously published in one or more standalone ebooks—and each is intended to stand alone here as well, meaning that you can read them in any order that appeals to you.

The common threads of people, technology, and workflow are integral to each section of the book, but each part homes in on one more specifically.

Part One examines the value of staff—not just in the abstract, but the quantifiable financial contributions employees make by improving service and productivity.

Part Two and Part Three look at details, metrics, and tools of workflow that can allow your people to be more productive, provide better service, and improve your bottom line.

Part Four looks at how modern practice marketing is driven largely by the internet—and how managing your online reputation is more important, but also easier, than you might realize.

And the last section, Part Five, looks closely at a selection of the most useful recent technologies to empower the practice business and improve efficiency, profitability and patient service.

I hope you enjoy this book and find it valuable. If you have feedback or would just like to connect, please email me at info@capko.com.

PART ONE

The People-Profit Connection:
Smart Staffing for Practice Profitability

Most practices are concerned about staff expenses and how they relate to profitability. That's not surprising. Staff payroll and benefits are often one of a practice's biggest expenses (if not the biggest). And as technology improves, it has the potential to make employees more productive–possibly allowing your practice to run not just better, but leaner.

Not having the right sized staff can undermine your profitability. But does it follow that minimizing staff is a reliable path to profitability?

Staffing for your best bottom line is not just a matter of keeping headcount to a minimum. Having *too few* staff can undercut profits, too. That problem is often much harder to spot—and can be much costlier.

This section of this book aims to help you think through your own staffing decisions looking not just at cost, but at profitability. We'll take a look at examples from my consulting experiences with Capko & Morgan, plus a tidbit or two from outside healthcare.

My hope is that when you take a closer look at how staff is deployed, you'll be keen to spot not just overstaffing, but also understaffing that can quietly erode your profits—and to find new ways to use staff, instead of trimming, that can actually strengthen your practice financially.

Failing to thrive? Subsistence staffing is not the answer

Here's something that might surprise you. When my partners and I consult for practices in financial trouble, it's rare to find them overstaffed. We're more likely to encounter understaffing than overstaffing when practices are struggling financially. Even when a practice is not making money, the core problem is rarely overstaffing.

Clients are often surprised when our recommendations don't focus on, or even include, cutting staff. But there is only so much profit that can be unlocked from trimming—and the gain is often temporary. What's more, staff cuts can cause problems that don't materialize for a while. These problems usually reduce profit by more than the wages that were saved. (By the time we're called in to help, problems caused by "savings" on staff may already be pulling a struggling practice further under water.)

Have you heard of the expression "a false economy"? It refers to an action that seems money-saving, but actually costs more in the long run. An everyday example is choosing a cheap set of tires that wears out more quickly than more expensive, higher quality ones. You save money initially, but you'll spend a lot more over time on replacing them more frequently.

One of the worst things about a false economy is that it takes a while to realize that your savings were not savings at all and have led to higher costs. Worse still, sometimes you never even figure out that you're losing money instead of saving. Trimming staff to the bone can be just like this. (And the consequences are much more costly than a new set of tires.)

Subsistence staffing—managing with the fewest possible employees—is just not the sure path to profitability it may seem to be. Employees don't only add costs; they do work that increases profitability, too. That's why it's not uncommon for us to recommend *adding* staff, even when working with a practice that's underperforming financially. Our recommendations usually focus on increasing revenue and productivity. To do that, you'll need to have enough staff on hand to help.

Practices are often surprised by this. Often they assume that generating more revenue is unlikely, maybe even impossible. But reconfiguring staff jobs and workflow, and sometimes adding new staff roles, can often yield higher productivity—and a better bottom line.

CASE STUDY: Overtime and profit potential

My partners and I recently worked with Dr. Alex Branson[1], an ambitious dermatologist and practice owner. Dr. Branson was bothered by the amount of overtime his practice was running up. He had just hired a new administrator and wanted us to analyze the overtime and develop a reasonable timeline for her to reduce expenses by eliminating it.

When we took a look at the practice's staffing and payroll data, we realized the physician was right to be concerned about the overtime. Nearly everyone on the staff was earning a significant amount of overtime. Several employees were earning more than 20% of their compensation in overtime! And about $60,000 in overtime per year was earned by just two nurses—each getting about 25% in pay above their base rate.

Dr. Branson felt that the main driver of overtime pay was employees "milking," especially while the practice was running without an administrator. (There had been a gap of about four months while the previous admin-

---

[1] While the case studies in this book draw on real experiences with actual practice clients, most of the names, locations, and other practice details that aren't relevant to the problems and outcomes have been anonymized for practice privacy. Some aspects of the cases have been simplified or amplified for clarity.

istrator was on leave before she eventually decided not to return.) He also assumed that reducing it was a matter of better scheduling rules and more management attention. He was focused on the immediate increase in profit he believed would come from simply cutting the overtime.

Why does overtime matter?

Dr. Branson's focus on the out-of-pocket cost of overtime was not unusual. The "premium pay" aspect of overtime expense gets a lot of attention in practice management literature. But there are often costlier problems than the pay premium itself when a practice runs up a lot of overtime.

The work being done in those extra hours, by fatigued employees, is usually done less well—so you're paying a higher wage for less productive time. And if everyone is consistently accruing overtime, it's likely there are other tasks that staff are too busy to get done at all[2]. High overtime can signal understaffing, workflow problems, scheduling problems—or a mix of all three. We expected that once we dug into the practice's data, we'd find more behind the overtime problem than opportunistic employees.

Benchmarks indicate understaffing

When we compared Dr. Branson's staffing to peer benchmarks, we found that the practice was very lean[3]—quite possibly too lean, especially in the back office. While the practice was profitable, the productivity of its five physicians was lower than its peer group—even though the practice offered services, such as Mohs surgery, that were in relatively short supply in its

---

[2]There are many studies exploring the connection between overtime, productivity, and errors. "The Effect of Work Hours on Adverse Events and Errors in Health Care," published in 2010 by Danielle Olds and Sean Clarke, is one recent, relevant one to check out.

[3]In this context I mean "lean," as in without a cushion, not "Lean," the statistical process control philosophy.

market. With their compensation based largely on productivity, we assumed that the doctors would have been willing to see more patients. It looked likely that their productivity was limited by their MA support.

There were other hints of understaffing besides the benchmarks. For example, online reviews included positive comments about the physicians, but there were negative ones about "stressed," "distracted," and "cranky" staff. There were other complaints about appointments falling behind schedule, and about how phones often went to voicemail.

The employee roster itself was another clue. Most of the practice's employees were new; only 20% had been with the practice longer than a year. Most of the jobs in the practice had been filled and refilled in the past three years. We also noticed that the practice had added two doctors in the past three years, but only one more staff role. If employees felt overtaxed due to understaffing, that could have contributed to this high turnover.

Overtime expense had been high for the past couple of years as well—not just during the period without an administrator. Employees may have come to resent the overtime if they were always expected to exceed their regular hours. (Not everyone loves working overtime, even at a higher wage. Many employees would prefer to work overtime only occasionally, so that it doesn't cut too deeply into free time.)

Scheduling, understaffing make overtime unavoidable

Then there was the conspicuous overtime of the two RNs. One nurse was an essential team member in the practice's surgery center. Since the practice had recently added another Mohs surgeon and part-time plastic surgeon, surgery days were always booked up with procedures from 7:30 to 5:00 or even 5:30. That meant that the nurse earned overtime each week by necessity, since she arrived before the first procedure and stayed until the last patient was able to leave. There was simply no way to cut her overtime without either changing the surgery schedule or adding RN help.

The second nurse supervised the back office in the practice's clinic and aesthetic center. While we couldn't be sure based just on the numbers, we suspected her overtime would also be hard to cut. Compared with survey data of dermatology practices, Dr. Branson's had a little more than half the average MA support per physician. His practice didn't seem to have nearly enough back office staff to keep patients flowing through efficiently. It looked like no more than one MA had been added in the past three years, even though two physicians had been added. We suspected that the nurse was pitching in on duties an MA could be doing and leaving her own paperwork and patient call-backs for after hours.

Of course, we were looking only at the numbers and not the practice workflow. There may, indeed, have been opportunities to improve the flow. But we were struck by the mix of very low staffing metrics and suppressed productivity we saw in the data. It strongly indicated that more support for the physicians and surgery center could deliver more profit than pushing the team to work faster while also cutting overtime.

Short-staffing is a false economy

The "savings" from not adding staff as quickly as the practice added physicians appeared to be a false economy. The practice saved on staff salaries and benefits, but now overtime was constantly required (at least for the RNs). Turnover was also adding costs—and probably was disruptive, too.

The data also suggested that the physicians were not getting nearly enough support to generate as much revenue as they could. If staff were added, that would add a bit to expenses, but could add much more revenue and bottom line profit by making the practice more productive.

Overtime issue

We shared our analysis with Dr. Branson, focusing on five points:

1. Overtime can be indicative of waste and bad habits, but not always.
2. Persistent overtime—especially in combination with turnover, low morale, and patient complaints—often indicates understaffing.
3. When people are routinely working overtime, the additional hours are probably less productive—so you pay more for less production.
4. Keeping staff too lean is a false economy, and not just because of overtime premium pay. Physicians need adequate support at every point in the workflow to maximize their productivity.
5. Based on benchmark and production data, we believed the practice was significantly understaffed. Consequently, we believed a lot of potential revenue and profit were being foregone.

Our recommendation: reframe the goal

Dr. Branson had framed the problem as overtime expense control, assuming that was the path to what he really wanted: more income. But by stating the problem that way, he unintentionally closed off solutions that would be more likely to increase profit—especially over the long haul.

Profit can be increased by growing the top line (revenue) or cutting expenses. There is only so much you can cut, though, and profit that comes from cutting expenses is often temporary. Growing revenue can be a clearer path to higher profit, since much overhead is fixed. Our first recommendation to Dr. Branson was to recast the goal as *more profit*, not expense reduction, to open the door to solutions besides squeezing the payroll.

Adding staff to add capacity

We had every indication that Dr. Branson's physicians and his surgery center could be more productive if they served more patients. To do that, we recommended that Dr. Branson *add* staff. Adding staff would increase the regular payroll, but it would reduce overtime. More important, with more support, the practice could increase revenue by much more than the added payroll expense.

They could start cautiously, with almost no risk, by first adding a part-time RN. The budget for the part-time nurse could be set to match the current surgery RN's overtime. That way, the cost would be a wash, but the practice would gain surgery capacity. They could then immediately expand the surgery schedule, bringing in more revenue and more profit.

The practice would also gain a bit of redundancy—breathing room, so that if a nurse was unexpectedly absent, surgery scheduling would not be completely disrupted. If, as we expected, the profit potential quickly became clear, the practice could next add more MAs to speed the flow in the clinic. These additions could also be funded mostly by the overtime saved. But the extra capacity in the clinic would allow all of the doctors to see more patients each day—immediately increasing profit.

It turned out to be harder to convince Dr. Branson than we expected[4]. We weren't surprised, though, even though we found the data quite convincing. Like many business-minded physicians, Dr. Branson had internalized a vivid picture of the dangers of overstaffing. Like so many doctors we work with, he had heard from many sources that anything but minimum staffing would automatically reduce profits. Even though the math was clear, he found it hard at first to embrace the idea that adding staff was actually less risky than continuing to operate without enough.

---

[4]Luckily, the new administrator looked at the workflow, saw the same staffing shortfalls we did, and made the same recommendation to Dr. Branson; they agreed to try hiring a new part-time RN—which they did right away, immediately improving productivity.

The costs of spending too much on practice staff are well-publicized (sometimes, in my opinion, almost to the point of fear-mongering). They're also easy to measure. The effect of understaffing, however, can be even more damaging to profitability. And understaffing not only gets a lot less attention, it's usually much harder to detect.

How did minimizing staff become a maxim? A theory

Long before I met my consulting partner Judy Capko, she had for years urged physicians to pay more attention to the value of staff. When she first began consulting in the late '80s and early '90s, she observed that many practices could quickly improve financial performance by taking better advantage of their staff's strengths.

Judy first developed this point of view in the early years of the managed care movement. At that time, her emphasis on staff contributions could almost have been described as contrarian. As managed care gained momentum, the going was rough for many practices. Revenues were squeezed, and physicians suddenly faced declining income. With few obvious options to increase revenue, many looked to cut costs. Staff expenses were usually the first place they looked. Staff became more "expendable."

For some practices, these were their first efforts to look critically at the business side. Some probably were overstaffed. But many others simply assumed it would be more profitable to make do with a smaller team, without really knowing for sure.

Of course, we all know what has happened in the decades since managed care took hold: continuous downward pressure on reimbursement. The constant threat of fee reductions has helped solidify the notion that minimizing staff costs is essential to profitability. But just because an assumption has become ingrained doesn't mean it's correct.

Revenues aren't fixed

I mentioned earlier that one reason physicians and managers tend to focus on expense cuts (and minimizing staff in particular) is that they assume revenue can't be increased[5]. That's unfortunate, because often revenue *can* be increased–and focusing on revenue often improves profits more quickly and more significantly than cost-cutting.

Yet there's an even more harmful assumption embedded in the focus on minimizing staff: the assumption that revenue *won't go down.*

If you've studied any economics, you've heard of the term "ceteris paribus." It means "all else being equal." It's a handy idea for envisioning how changes in a single variable can affect an economic outcome.

Let's say, for example, that you have built a popular ice pop business. Summer is coming, and you'd like to find a way to improve your profits. You investigate and discover that cheaper flavorings are available. If you reduce the flavorings cost in your spreadsheet and change nothing else, your profits will increase by the amount of your cost savings. Right?

Well, as economists like to say, it depends. Ceteris paribus, your profits would improve. But in real life, things are rarely as easily calculated.

What if, for example, the cheaper flavorings don't taste as good as the originals? Demand may drop—especially if competitors' frozen snacks now taste better than yours. If you can't sell as many pops, you could earn more profit per pop, but less overall profit.

---

[5]Sadly this, too, may be a vestige of the upheaval created when managed care emerged. It's tough for some doctors and managers to imagine anything but steadily declining revenue. But productivity can improve revenues and profitability.

Ceteris paribus is a great tool to understand the basics of how a single piece contributes to an economic puzzle. But if you make it an assumption in real planning—like swapping a key ingredient without knowing its importance to the customer—it can cause a lot of trouble.

In the case of practice staffing, it's tempting to assume that cutting staff only affects the expense line on the spreadsheet, and so immediately improves profitability. But cutting staff may not be—in fact, probably isn't—a ceteris paribus decision.

Go even a little too lean and service and capacity will decline, even if the degradation takes a while to detect. Slight decreases in service quality, for example, may not show up in online reviews for a few months or more. Productivity may erode gradually, just a visit or two less per month at first; it might be a year or two before the trend is clear. By that time, it can be more difficult to figure out what the problem is—and more costly to fix it.

Getting by with less help—or are they?

My partners and I have worked with practices that were very proud to have minimized back office staff—noting that they've discovered they can "get by easily" with fewer MAs. But how, exactly, are they getting by? And are they really getting by?

Consider this hypothetical example[6].

A practice employs an MA floater, who works alongside a team of MAs who each directly support one of five physicians. The floater covers

---

[6]It's a hypothetical case, but every included decision, snag, and unintended consequence is something my partners and I have seen in a real practice.

absences; ensures all rooms are cleaned and identically stocked; pitches in to relieve bottlenecks during rushes; and monitors patient flow from front to back, to be sure no one's missed or left waiting too long.

The practice's diligent administrator is highly motivated to improve practice efficiency. (It's not just her natural inclination: she's been promised a bonus if she can cut waste.) She looks at the floater's tasks and decides they can easily be absorbed by others. She also notices that everyone has at least a few minutes each hour when they don't appear to be busy.

"Everyone has slack time during the day, and that's wasteful," she reasons. "If we eliminate the floater, that's $35,000 or so right to the bottom line. The front desk can watch for patients who've been waiting too long. We'll make sure the other MAs know how to stock and clean their rooms properly. We just need to get everyone working a bit more productively."

So the job is eliminated, and things seem to have sorted themselves out fine, at least at first. Or have they?

The receptionists had plenty of work to do before they were asked to "just keep an eye out" for patients who'd been waiting too long—and they know their primary tasks are more important. The daily metrics they're measured on tell them what matters most: copay collection, emails captured, insurance cards scanned. So sure, they'll keep an eye out—when they have nothing more pressing to do.

Even when they notice a patient has been waiting too long, the receptionists may not be able to address the problem. They can't see what's causing a delay in back from their desks in the front. They can ask the physician's MA for help—but if the doctor is backed up, the MA likely is too (especially now that the MAs no longer have the floater's help).

So what used to be a primary responsibility for the floating MA becomes an if-you-have-time responsibility for the front desk. Patients waiting too long are less likely to be spotted, and even if someone notices, they won't be able to help. Extra delays and less attention don't impact every patient, but the number having this unpleasant experience increases.

Back office workflow takes a hit, too. With their MAs busier, the doctors now occasionally have to step out of the exam room for missing supplies. Sometimes they get behind because no room is ready, or because no one was available to escort their patient. They may eventually even get into the habit of fetching their patients themselves sometimes, to avoid falling further behind. And then when everyone's slightly increased workload puts the entire clinic behind, perhaps they even find themselves hoping for a no-show or two to catch up.

These little problems are easy to overlook in the short run. (In fact, they may look at first like temporary adjustment problems. Or even success: If everyone is busier, doesn't that mean they're better utilized?)

But, gradually, less attentive service leads to disappointed or frustrated patients. And that leads to fewer referrals, more complaints, even attrition—and that means higher marketing costs.

Less support in the back office also lowers the ceiling on physician productivity. Productivity losses that are too small to notice day-to-day eventually become measurable, just more slowly than the immediate "savings" from cutting staff. Even just one fewer visit per day for the entire clinic could almost negate the $35,000 saved by cutting an MA—and the reduction in throughput could easily end up being much greater than that.

The practice likely incurs more overtime costs, too. Even just a little more overtime here, a little more there will quickly offset much of the savings from the lost headcount.

And what if the MA floater had not been let go? Instead of focusing on cutting costs, the administrator could instead have attempted to increase weekly visits to improve profitability. This would have required more analysis and creativity, but could have brought in much more than $35,000 in new annual revenue.

A little slack prevents bigger problems

Mistaking activity for productivity can do great damage to patient flow, patient service, and profitability[7].

This idea can be very counterintuitive when you look out of your office door and see staff with idle time. If you're a motivated, energetic person, it can be hard not to see any staff downtime as a cost. But zero slack is an unrealistic goal. What's more, striving for it can actually be more costly to your practice than a little bit of downtime.

When everyone is running at full speed 100% of the time, some tasks are probably not getting done—or are not being done as well as they should be. And there is no room to stretch, so when an unexpected need or sudden surge of demand occurs, it can lead to more errors and unnecessary stress.

Even practices that excel at analyzing their scheduling and peak load times will find there are still some events that cause unpredictable waves—a particularly bad flu season, a drug recall that prompts nervous calls, emergencies that pull a doctor away from the clinic, etc. Problems like a network or software outage can also cause a sudden temporary increase in everyone's workload. And, of course, there are smaller, daily variations, like visits that just take a bit longer than expected, or a team member's illness or emergency.

---

[7]We'll be exploring this idea further in Part Three.

Having enough extra staff capacity to stretch to accommodate these situations, without sacrificing patient service or other trade-offs, helps insure your practice against patient attrition. With enough staff to stretch, you'll be able to handle the surge without excess errors, incomplete tasks, or turning patients away. (That last one is vitally important not just to your mission, but to competitiveness and profitability. Patients need to know you'll be there when they need you.)

Surges are revenue opportunities, too. Being able to handle them in stride is an opportunity to bring more money through the door.

On the flip side, if you staff with the goal that everyone will always be busy, even during normal or relatively slow periods, then even a small unexpected increase in activity will be much harder to absorb. Work will be done less well—sometimes in ways that aren't immediately obvious, but that quietly cost money. When practice managers and physicians focus on reducing idle time instead of job content or workflow needs, a tipping point can quickly be reached where productivity and/or quality are silently but steadily degraded.

Here's just one common example. If your front desk is overloaded, perhaps details like checking IDs, insurance, or address information; collecting copays; or collecting email or text contact information are not handled 100% of the time.

These seem like small tasks. But when they're not done at check-in, problems and costs result downstream. Unverified information can cause billing problems, copays become uncollectable, or opportunities to save postage and time with electronic statements are missed. Because these problems happen much later in the workflow, it can be hard to tie them back to understaffing at the front desk. Worse, their costs can quickly exceed the cost of adding a bit more help.

Visualizing the workflow tipping point: Lucy's assembly line

(Image source: YouTube.com)

The famous *I Love Lucy* episode "Job Switching," which features Lucy and Ethel's attempts to master a candy assembly line job, playfully illustrates how even small increases in demand can quickly derail performance when employees are already at capacity.

(If you're young enough that you haven't seen it, take a couple of moments to watch one of the clips on YouTube.com, or the entire episode at CBS.com—I promise you'll enjoy it. Actually, even if you have seen it before, why not watch it again right now? It's just a couple of minutes long, and it's a lot of fun.)

In the scene, Lucy and Ethel must pick candy from a conveyor, wrap it, and then replace it on the belt for packaging later down the line. "If one piece of candy gets past you and into the packing room unwrapped," bellows the boss, *"you're fired!"*

Despite being nervous about screwing up, as the line slowly starts, Lucy and Ethel initially manage well. But just moments later the pace increases—and they quickly fall far behind. They desperately try to avoid sending unwrapped candies down the line by removing them and piling them up, eating them, even stuffing them into their pockets and hats.

Of course it's exaggerated for humor, but the scene offers a great operations management demo. It illustrates a point about staffing and capacity that can be very hard to visualize. Overloading the process impacts both quality and quantity. When the pace increases beyond Lucy and Ethel's capacity, not only is some of the work not getting done at all, the work that is getting done is done much more sloppily as the workers become frantic in their efforts to keep up.

Employees aim to please—to a fault

The boss's behavior is another source of comedy—an exaggerated example of what not to do. When she stops the line to check on Lucy and Ethel, they've already scrambled to hide all the evidence of how poorly they're doing. The boss overlooks the candies shoved into clothing and mouths—and concludes that the line should move even faster! Determined not to be fired, Lucy and Ethel pretend that all is going fine.

In real life, a factory supervisor worth her salt would have no excuse for not observing the line while it's actually moving. But it's easy to see how the nature of a physician's job makes this a much more common and challenging pitfall for a practice.

Most of medical office workflow happens when physicians are in exam rooms—unable to see or analyze what's happening. Moreover, employees are often reluctant to disappoint their physicians or their managers. It's crucial to remember that just because employees are eager to please does not mean they have excess capacity. Even when they're maxed out, employees will often be reluctant to admit that things are slipping, or that they're having trouble keeping up.

Communication and trust are key

Of course, this is where trusted relationships between physicians and managers can make all the difference. Managers and administrators need to be able to accurately evaluate the positive and negative impact of staff cuts and additions, and be honest about what they find.

Trusted employee-manager relationships are critical, too. Employees need to be able to speak up when overtaxed, without fear that it will cost them their jobs. Otherwise, excess stress can lead to poor morale, which can impact the patient experience. And it will eventually lead to turnover and its costs, including recruitment, overtime or temp help, administrative attention diverted to hiring, background checking, on-boarding paperwork, and new employee training.

Benefits of slack: lessons from retail

In 2008, Zeynep Ton, DBA, published a paper at the Harvard Business School entitled, "The Effect of Labor on Profitability: the Role of Quality."[8] Dr. Ton observed in retail, as I have in medical practices, that the costs of adding labor are significant and easy to measure, while the benefits are "indirect and not immediately felt."[9] This helps explain why most of the attention to staffing in both retail and healthcare focuses on minimizing headcount. Yet in her research, Dr. Ton was able to show how having a bit of "extra" staff actually increases profitability. She was also able to identify and quantify those bottom-line benefits.

---

[8] Ton's research is online at: http://www.hbs.edu/faculty/Publication%20Files/09-040_146640ac-c502-4c2a-9e97-f8370c7c6903.pdf. Or read her book, The Good Jobs Strategy, which expanded on this research.

[9] "The Effect of Labor on Profitability: The Role of Quality," Zeynep Ton, 2008, p.3.

Dr. Ton learned that having a staff cushion in retail settings helps improve "conformance quality"—meaning how fully and accurately staff completes tasks. Just as in medical practices, workload can be unpredictable in retail; having a bit of slack ensures employees always have capacity to provide good service and complete tasks properly.

When a retail establishment has a bit more staff than it could get by with, work doesn't have to be redone as often. There are fewer losses from mistakes, and tasks aren't left unfinished. The costs of these errors and omissions are less obvious on the surface, which is one reason it always seems like a good idea to get by with as few people as you can. But Ton's research was able to show how, over time, having a bit of slack in staffing helps retail companies earn more by avoiding mistakes that quietly cut profitability.

Retail operations have several key things in common with practices, staffing-wise. There are a lot of tasks that need to be done by humans, not machines, in both settings. Staff is one of the biggest expenses, so the instinct to minimize personnel comes naturally—and is hard to fight. Employees have the potential to add tremendously to the customer experience in retail and the patient experience in healthcare (or to detract from it). And in both settings, employee errors can create significant costs that aren't always apparent—that is, the conformance quality impact that Dr. Ton's research identified.

It's also true of both settings that, on the margin, each additional staffer is not enormously expensive. Entry level roles in retail and in healthcare are relatively low-paying. This is another reason the profit impact of, say, an "extra" medical assistant (or store clerk) can be so positive.

In our consulting work, our 30,000 foot view of a practice lets us see how conformance quality affects profitability as workflow proceeds. Small omissions and errors in scheduling and at the front desk cause problems in billing, where they are more expensive to fix (or possibly not fixable at all, costing even more). Small front office delays can be the hidden cause of bottlenecks that put practices behind schedule, causing them to schedule fewer total patients. Missed instructions to patients about follow-up visits by rushed MAs create more phone calls weeks later—or lost revenue and increased risk due to skipped visits. The "savings" from having one or two fewer employees can quickly be wiped out by these costs (as we'll explore in detail in an upcoming case study).

Dr. Ton's research also looked at "service quality"—how well customers are served. She found that it also improved, but that for retail operations, the impact on profit wasn't measurable. But for medical practices, with patient assessments becoming more tied to reimbursement and patients increasingly sharing their opinions and experiences, we can reasonably expect service quality to eventually impact profit. Dr. Ton's paper noted that research specific to healthcare has connected service quality and profitability[10]. Knowing that service can be measurably boosted with a fuller staff is another good reason to rethink keeping staff as lean as possible.

How to be overstaffed and underproductive: the mirage of multitasking

Overtime is one way practices to try "get by" with fewer staff than the practice needs to function at its best. Another is to assign more tasks to each role and to expect employees to multitask.

Multitasking seems like a staffing bargain. Theoretically, if employees would otherwise have a few moments of idle time, multitasking makes

---

[10]In "The Effect of Labor on Profitability," Dr. Ton cites a 1992 study by Nelson, et al, of 51 hospitals. This study found that service quality in hospitals is correlated with revenue, earnings, and return on assets.

them fully productive. This is one reason so many practices are still tempted to have front desk staff responsible for both patients checking in and out of the practice and for answering the phone.

If you've been at the front desk in a busy practice that uses this approach, you can attest that the receptionists are certainly busy. But is this more productive than allowing them to focus on the patients in front of them?

Research—and simple intuition—says no. While combining these tasks might all-but-eliminate idle time, that doesn't necessarily mean higher productivity. That's because trying to do two or more different sorts of tasks at the same time is taxing for the brain. You're actually not doing two tasks simultaneously—you're switching between them as quickly as your brain can manage. But each time you switch from one focus to another, your brain requires a pause to regroup, and that cuts into productivity. One study[11] found that as much as 40 percent of potential productivity is lost when employees are asked to frequently switch.

If you're asking employees to do a lot of multitasking instead of allowing them to focus, it's likely you're getting a lot less productivity than you could from your team. Even with plenty of staff you could be underproductive, because multitasking employees aren't able to give their best.

But worst of all, when we see stressed-out employees burdened with a lot of multitasking, it's usually in combination with understaffing. That's because multitasking looks like a way to get more work done with fewer people. Unfortunately, the opposite is true. Having too few employees, then asking them to juggle multiple responsibilities in real time, is a sure-fire path to even *lower* productivity than with understaffing alone.

---

[11] Read about the research at the American Psychological Association website, http://www.apa.org/research/action/multitask.aspx.

As we'll explore in the next section, the impact of too few employees and too much multitasking can play out disastrously, especially for independent practices. To stand alone, practices need to have enough people and set them up to be productive. Having enough staff can also allow smaller practices to provide the kind of excellent service that will stand out versus larger healthcare organizations.

Staffing well is more important in an independent practice setting

My consulting partners and I have found that physician-owners of independent practices are often especially anxious about overstaffing. They have absorbed all the warnings about how excess staff cuts into profits. And they perceive that any excess expense will jeopardize practice profitability—hitting them in the pocketbook personally. They're also often unaware of the risks of understaffing, or how it can be especially problematic in an independent practice.

Unlike a group within a large system, there's no chance of an independent practice "borrowing" well-trained help temporarily from another part of the organization to weather a sudden surge. The same is true if an employee unexpectedly resigns or needs to take a leave. All key business functions—from scheduling, to insurance verification and authorization, to billing and collections—are the responsibility of the practice. Not having enough help in any area can cause problems much more quickly than in a larger organization.

One of the clearest advantages an independent practice has is the opportunity to stand out from larger organizations with more personalized, attentive service. But when understaffing nibbles away at the personal touch, independent practices lose the very thing that gives their organizations a significant advantage versus large systems and hospitals. And when an independent practice's staff is insufficient to respond quickly, patients may lose confidence that the practice can meet their needs, even when the problems have nothing to do with clinical skill.

CASE STUDY: Understaffing derails a start-up practice

We worked with a new, independent rheumatology practice recently that was learning these lessons the hard way. The managing partner, Dr. Rose, had never led a practice before, but was interested in business and eager to take charge. She also believed she'd spotted inefficiencies in her practice's previous situation within an integrated health system. When she and her three partners stepped out on their own, Dr. Rose was determined that they would not to repeat those errors.

What stood out most to Dr. Rose at the integrated system was that staff seemed idle a lot. She was convinced they had been overstaffed. But what she couldn't see was that many important tasks were not being done. Overstaffing was not the reason staff had downtime; badly defined jobs and lack of attention from centralized management were actually to blame.

Besides misinterpreting the idle time, Dr. Rose didn't realize how much work was handled by the system's centralized billing and customer service teams. This caused her to underestimate her new practice's staff needs even more. She counted the number of receptionists and back office MAs she and her partners had in the integrated system, subtracted a few headcount, and used that as her total roster for the new practice. She was convinced that a smaller number of staff could do it all. She wanted to be sure there was no idle time, and was convinced everyone could do more through multitasking.

An ounce of prevention, ignored

Nine months earlier, Dr. Rose and her partners had asked Capko & Morgan for help creating a plan for their new practice. Our plan included a staff roster that would allow the practice to run smoothly. But there were several positions that Dr. Rose argued could be omitted in favor of combining roles and multitasking.

We strongly urged the four partners to stick with our recommendations, which were based on both our experiences with many rheumatology practices as well as survey benchmark data. We ended the project believing we had persuaded them. But now, many months later, we learned that Dr. Rose had ultimately insisted on her stripped-down staffing plan. The baby practice was now in serious trouble, overwhelmed by avoidable workflow problems created by understaffing.

Dr. Rose had most strongly disagreed with our recommendations about the phones. She wanted the front desk to handle phones as well as check patients in and out. We had explained that a mini call center for phone triage and scheduling was a proven best practice. Multitasking at the front desk leads to stress, errors, and a disappointing experience for both the patients on the phone and the ones in reception. But Dr. Rose was more concerned that the receptionists might not be utilized 100% of the time if they didn't also answer phones.

The call team would have ensured the practice duplicated the centralized scheduling support they'd gotten at the integrated system. We explained that their four-doctor practice would receive a lot of calls, especially since patients had no other way to schedule. Patients could be in severe pain or dealing with medication issues, making answering promptly more important. Patients the doctors had seen for years would now be "new" to the practice, which would mean longer calls that would be even harder to manage at reception. The phones were an absolutely crucial point of patient service and the starting point of patient flow. They had to be staffed well for the practice to succeed.

The other partners seemed to agree with us. We had emphasized that the costs of adding a couple of schedulers were relatively small–especially in comparison to the cost of a breakdown in scheduling and phone service. But in the months after we finished the planning process, Dr. Rose returned to her view that calls could be handled by the receptionists. "They won't always be busy," she argued. Dr. Rose could see only the potential for idle time if they hired dedicated phone staff, and she intensely feared what she saw as "wasted money."

Doors open; avoidable meltdown ensues

The practice had many patients booked starting the day they opened their doors. The disastrous impact of Dr. Rose's staffing decisions was apparent almost immediately. Overwhelmed receptionists were trying to check patients in and out while handling often-lengthy calls. Calls went unanswered. Voicemails piled up.

We arrived at the new practice two months after opening day. Many problems had escalated to crisis level. The first thing we noticed was the phones: they were ringing constantly. The practice also had a persistent backlog of unheard voicemails. As the staff cleared some messages, even more poured in. Longstanding patients couldn't connect to re-establish their routine visits.

The doctors were understandably exasperated by the ringing phones and concerned about voicemails accumulating. So they would demand– sometimes angrily—that phones be answered immediately. But then when the practice's two receptionists were occupied on calls, no one could check patients in. Patients stood in motionless lines at the reception desk, watching in frustration as staff stopped check-ins to answer calls.

Major bottlenecks disrupted the workflow. Doctors paced the floor in the back, while their patients waited grumpily in line in reception. All the chairs were frequently occupied, and patients, often in pain, had to stand.

The atmosphere was a lot like Lucy and Ethel's panicked hiding of the chocolates on the assembly line—chaotic, stressful, a bit crazy. (But, of course, no one was laughing.) Everyone was working overtime every day. Mistakes and costs were piling up, and morale was in tatters. Important work was not getting done. The doctors were frustrated and angry, patients were unhappy, and staff felt like they were failing.

There was, unfortunately, plenty of yelling, blaming, and tears.

This was one of the toughest situations my partners and I had ever seen. Worst of all, most of the pain could have been avoided.

The solution is obvious: or is it?

Of course, this case study, while based on a real practice, is an extreme example. But it helps illustrate how costly understaffing can be in an independent practice. Workflow can spiral out of control very, very fast. There's no main office to go to for help. And there's nothing that can be done in the heat of the moment but to hang tough and try to get all the work done.

Once the practice brought us in, we could see immediately how the problems could be easily fixed with a few more staff. But as obvious as it was to us, we still had a hard time convincing Dr. Rose.

Even with compelling evidence that understaffing was handicapping her new practice, Dr. Rose was still *more* afraid of overstaffing. Guarding against that fear of overstaffing was hurting the practice financially much more than an extra employee or two ever could have.

Quantifying costs provides a perspective

The only way to make our case to Dr. Rose and her partners was with data. Dr. Rose had an intense vision of the money to pay more staff coming out of her pocket, but she couldn't see that not having enough staff was hitting her wallet even harder. Our job was to make those costs visible.

Qualified front and back office MAs could be easily found in the local market at an average cost of $23/hour, including benefits and taxes. For the front office, our recommended additions—two full-time schedulers, plus a half-time floater for scheduling and reception—would add about $2,200 per week to the payroll, or about $114,000 per year. Now we needed to quickly quantify the impact of the problems these employees could solve, to show that they cost the practice more than that.

We could see numerous ways understaffing the front office added costs. We started with three of the easiest to quantify: the higher cost of answering voicemails versus live calls; the potential for patient attrition; and missing billing details at scheduling and check-in.

- *Work generated by voicemails versus handling calls live*
Handling a call as it comes in typically takes one to ten minutes. (Dr. Rose's practice still had some calls that took 12-15 minutes, because the practice was new. More data needed to be captured, and patients usually needed driving directions. But one to ten minutes is a good rule of thumb.) When the call goes to voicemail, additional time is needed to listen to the message and make note of how to handle it. The practice was averaging about 30-40 new voicemails accumulated, unheard, at the end of each day. Assuming an average of one to two minutes per voicemail, the practice had accumulated *three to four hours* of extra work per week just to listen to voicemail.

Calling patients back also takes longer than answering inbound calls does. Some patients won't be available to answer and will be called more than once. Dr. Rose said she believed that one-third of the voicemails were repeat callers, meaning 20-30 per day required a call-back. Assuming, conservatively, an average of five minutes per call, that meant about 10 hours per week of call-backs.

Together, the tasks of listening to voicemails and calling patients back represented about 13 hours per week that wasn't being done. Since the work couldn't be completed during regular hours, we factored in an overtime premium of 50% of the $17.25 base wage. At about $31.50 per hour and 13 hours per week, the cost of voicemails accumulating due to short-staffing was running about $21,380 per year in extra hours. This meant that just the task of managing voicemail justified half of the cost of a scheduler.

● *Patient attrition*

Dr. Rose thought the fact that one-third of the calls were repeats meant that the number of missed calls was "not as bad as it seemed." But patients who call back repeatedly are patients the practice is at risk of losing to competitors. Plus, for every voicemail received, there are other patients who are uncomfortable leaving a message. Some patients who don't get through to a person and get tired of leaving messages, or who simply need to see a rheumatologist more quickly, will decide it's time to find another doctor.

The financial impact of repeat and abandoned calls can be huge. After observing the practice and reviewing available phone log data, we estimated that, in addition to the 150 callers who left voicemails each week, there were another 100 abandoned calls. Some portion of these abandoners will give up and look for another rheumatologist.

What would the cost be of this attrition? A rheumatology patient is typically seen several times per year. Many patients receive infusion therapies that require more follow-up, and which generate administration revenue for the practice. Even estimating conservatively, we projected that the average value of a patient who left the practice would be at least $400 in revenue per year.

At this rate, if even 2% of the missed calls led the patient to look for another practice, Dr. Rose and her colleagues were giving up two patients per week, or $800—a loss rate of $40,000 per year. (This includes only lost revenue, not the hard costs of attrition, including the need to replace lost patients through marketing.)

- *Missed billing details*

The receptionists had primary responsibility for answering calls. They took most of the calls that were successfully answered, juggling them with check-in and check-out. The receptionists had some training in gathering insurance information and verifying coverage when scheduling, but not much. They'd come right out of training or from practices where receptionists didn't handle scheduling, so it was all new to them. Plus, they were overwhelmed and stressed, with impatient patients waiting in front of them to check in.

Because of all these factors, details were missed and verifications were mostly skipped. (Sometimes back office MAs pitched in to answer a few calls. They were even less familiar with collecting patient information!)

The missing verifications and patient demographic data created huge problems at the practice's billing service. Some of the patients didn't realize they were now out-of-network and would pay more out of pocket. Others could not expect their coverage to apply at all. The billing service estimated that nearly a third of visits could not even be billed until information was either supplemented or corrected.

At such an early stage of the practice's life, it was difficult to gauge the impact of so many delayed claims, probable denials, and rework. The billing service team was anxious. They knew that cash flow would be slow to come, and some claims would surely be dead if these problems were not corrected.

A more immediate and measurable cash crunch was caused by copays and deductibles. In setting its startup budget, the practice had expected that copays and other collections at the front desk would provide vital, immediate revenue. But the receptionists had little time to collect (much less calculate the amounts due) while trying to juggle patients waiting anxiously in line and constantly ringing phones.

We observed about 90% of the patients being told, "We'll bill you for any copay or deductible." The billing service said that on average three statement mailings–at $.75 each–would be required to collect in full. For the 60-70 patients currently booked daily, the paper and postage expense alone would run more than $30,000 per year.

Even that statement cost was small, though, compared to a bigger risk of not collecting patient payments at the time of service: the risk the practice might never be paid at all. The billing service estimated that as much as 15% of balances billed to patients would likely need to be written off eventually. Between copays and deductible amounts, the average amount per patient that should have been collected at the time of service was over $60. This meant that the practice was risking about $3,000 per week in write-offs—or $150,000 per year.

The impact of understaffing on front desk collections was clearly huge. And this didn't even incorporate the extra labor required to reenter demographic information and try to resubmit claims—or the costs of patients accidentally seen for uncovered services.

These three areas alone were on pace to cost the practice more than $250,000 annually—and these were just the most obvious costs. Adding the needed front office staff at a cost of $114,000 would deliver more than double that amount in collections and avoided expenses. Plus, that return didn't even include the gains to be made in patient service, and especially in workflow. Improving the workflow and reducing the bottlenecks currently plaguing reception would allow the practice to increase the doctors' productivity and generate a lot more revenue.

Restoring a doctor's superior productivity

To help immediately increase revenue, we recommended at least one back office MA be hired to increase support for Dr. Goodman. Dr. Goodman's productivity had been much higher at the integrated system. But under Dr. Rose's tighter staffing plan, he was only allowed one MA, not two like he had previously. This had slowed him down considerably. The immediate financial impact was easy to estimate.

At the integrated system, Dr. Goodman had regularly seen 30-40 patients per day—high for rheumatology—but he was now working overtime to complete about 20 visits per day. He was still seeing more patients than the other three doctors—especially Dr. Rose, who was spending a lot of time acting as the practice administrator. But he was frustrated to be unable to move at his normal pace.

For years Dr. Goodman had relied on two skilled MAs to help him maintain his superior pace. They had been a well-tuned team. Now, under Dr. Rose's strict expense budgeting, he was trying to keep up with just a single MA. That MA, in turn, was working at least one to two hours overtime every day.

Restoring the set-up that had enabled Dr. Goodman to hit such a high productivity standard would bring in much needed revenue. And it was obvious that more support—combined with front office improvements speeding up the flow from check-in to rooming—could help get Dr. Goodman closer to his normal pace. He'd be happier, and the practice would be significantly more productive. (Not to mention the benefits to his patients, many of whom were trying desperately to get in to see him.)

We estimated, conservatively, that Dr. Goodman could immediately see at least seven more patients per day with an additional MA. (We knew that his productivity could and should be even higher, based on his history—and that it would continue to improve. But the front office would also need to be more effective for him to reach his previous capacity.)

We also worked with conservative assumptions on reimbursement. We assumed only an office visit was charged for each new patient. And we assumed a blend of new and established patients, all at level three, with about 80% coded at 99213. The math worked out as follows:

Additional visits:	at least 35/week
Average reimbursement:	$80/visit
Additional revenue:	at least $2,800/week
Cost of 2nd MA:	$920/week
Less current MA's overtime: ($170)/week	
Minimum added profit:	at least $2,050/week or $98,400/48 weeks

These calculations were conservative in assuming Dr. Goodman would reach 27-30 visits per day with the additional help. As the entire practice workflow as a whole improved, Dr. Goodman could add another five or more visits per day, potentially doubling the additional profit (especially since we excluded other revenue generating services like infusions from our math for simplicity).

Once Dr. Goodman's practice was running more smoothly (and generating much-needed revenue), we also recommended an MA floater be added to provide more support for the other three doctors to help improve their productivity and serve patients better. We estimated—conservatively—that the floater could enable the other three doctors to add at least 15 visits per week. Plus, the floater would enable the other MAs to complete their tasks without overtime.

Calculated with the same assumptions as for Dr. Goodman's added MA, the floater's profit impact would be:

Additional visits:	at least 15/week
Average reimbursement:	$80/visit
Additional revenue:	at least $1,200/week
Cost of 2nd MA:	$920/week
Less current MAs' overtime:	($170)/week x 3 = ($510)
Minimum added profit:	at least $810/week or $38,800/48 weeks

Pulling the numbers together—ROI on staff investments

Toted up, these numbers paint a picture of the added staff as an *investment*—not just an expense. And even though we looked just at the most immediate, easily measured gains, the picture was still extremely compelling:

Front office payroll increase:	$114,000/year
Costs avoided:	
Voicemail OT:	$ 21,380/year
Patient attrition:	$ 40,000/year
Statement costs (copays):	$ 30,000/year
Likely balance write-offs:	$150,000/year
Front office investment ROI:	$127,380/year

Back office payroll increase
  (net of overtime avoided): $60,320/year

Increased profit (Goodman): $98,400/year
Increased profit (others): $38,800/year

Back office investment ROI: $76,880/year

Total staff investment ROI: $204,260/year

One additional recommendation

There was one further recommendation we made to Dr. Rose and her practice partners: We recommended they bring in a full-time, experienced administrator. Dr. Rose was spending more and more of her time trying to manage staff and run the business operations of the practice. But Dr. Rose was a complete newbie to management, and there was no one to mentor her. The practice also needed full-time management, but Dr. Rose was still trying to maintain her normal patient load while running the practice business as a "side job."

There was also an enormous opportunity cost to her involvement with managing the practice. As a physician, she could generate at least $200-$300 per hour in revenue. Instead, she was doing work that a practice manager could do better, and at much lower cost.

An experienced administrator could bring invaluable skills and expertise that would help the practice grow much more steadily in the coming years. And it was likely that the entire cost of adding an administrator would be offset by Dr. Rose's return to normal productivity.

Staffing costs versus physician opportunity costs

In its 2014 *Performance and Practices of Successful Medical Groups* report, the MGMA found that the most profitable practices of the 2,518 it surveyed had significantly more staff per physician than average. The top performers in the study had an average of 6.33 support staff per physician, versus 4.31 at other practices.

These data don't just show that adequate staff is essential to profitability. Just as Zeynep Ton's study showed for retail, the MGMA data showed that having more staff in comparison to practice peers can be a *profitability advantage*.

As Dr. Ton's study described, a staffing cushion helps practices protect conformance quality—things get done, and they get done right. But in a medical practice there is another huge contribution that staff makes to practice profitability: enabling the physicians they support to be as productive as they can be.

Consider the hourly cost of an employed physician, PA/NP, nurse, or MA. The employed physician might cost anywhere from $100-$300 per hour (or more, depending on specialty); the PA/NP $45-$60 per hour; the nurse $25-35 per hour; and the MA, $10-$20 per hour. Every time a physician or PA/NP does the work of an MA, the practice in effect pays a wage that's 5-10x the price for that work. Cutting staff to the point where physicians and other clinicians find themselves "pitching in" on MA tasks themselves—even occasionally—means paying physician wages for MA work.

Ouch, right? Actually, it's even worse than that.

Hard costs plus opportunity costs

Clinician time is the practice's billable resource. When physicians, physician assistants (PAs), nurse practitioners (NPs), and other nonphysician providers (NPPs) do tasks a staff member could do, the practice foregoes the revenue that clinician could have generated in that time. If a physician spends even an hour a week on tasks staff could do instead, the practice could lose $200-$300 or more in revenue—plus the expenses of having the physician on staff. The total loss could be $400 or $500 or more.

The missed revenue is what economists call an opportunity cost. The most economically valuable use of a physician's time is seeing patients—the opportunity cost is the cost of doing something else instead.[12]

Now consider the converse. If an additional MA could take even an hour or two of tasks off a physician's plate per week, the cost quickly "pencils out" —and that's before the other benefits of adding that staff member are even contemplated.

Of course, a single staff member could likely take more than an hour's worth of tasks off several physicians' plates. Plus, that employee's efforts could mean the difference between adequate and noteworthy service. That extra set of hands could provide the slack needed to ensure that ebbs and flows in demand don't snowball into costly problems. And in specialties like dermatology, plastic surgery, or integrative medicine, an extra staff member might even help sell retail products or elective services.

Technology changes the game

If you've seen one of my recent articles or webinars, you already know that I'm an enthusiastic fan of the new wave of technology available to support practice operations (as you'll see in detail in Part Five). Tasks like collecting from patients, reminding them about follow-up care, verify-

---

[12]It probably goes without saying that the clinicians themselves incur a personal cost, since they'd also prefer to focus on patient care and not be distracted by tasks MAs can do for them.

ing insurance, and scheduling appointments can all be managed better with new tech solutions. Making these tasks more efficient can deliver immediate profitability benefits to practices.

But whenever we work with a practice that's considering automating some office tasks, the fear of overstaffing usually surfaces. When technology makes a practice more efficient, does that mean it needs less staff?

Of course, like any good undergraduate economics major, my first response is, "It depends." For sure, though, there are probably many more profitable steps to look at first, before even contemplating cutting staff.

Technology requires people, too

Technology has the power to do great things for your practice, but it requires knowledgeable people to use it. If you don't have enough staff, or staff that are experienced and well-trained enough, you won't get the most out of any technology implementation.

One of the things we notice in most practices we work with is that the technology they already have is at least partially underutilized.

In the competitive electronic health record (EHR) and, especially, practice management system (PMS) markets, vendors are rolling out new features all the time. (This is especially true with cloud-based systems.) In the constant daily flood of email, important announcements and training opportunities get missed—especially when a busy physician or administrator is the only person empowered to receive and act on them.

The variety of missed features we've seen—benefits practices have paid for, but don't know are available—is huge. For just a few examples, we've worked with practice teams that didn't know about insurance card scanners that plug into their PMS, didn't realize they could set up a payment portal in minutes, and had no idea that superbill information could be shared automatically from their EHR to PMS.

Adding newer technologies that put a bit of slack back into your operations offers the opportunity to take a fresh look at how your jobs are configured. Employees who are well-hired, well-trained, and empowered can help ensure your practice takes full advantage of your tech investments.

Rooting out waste

When physicians and managers think about trimming staff, what they're really concerned about is waste—a valid concern. But waste can occur in many other parts of a practice besides staffing. Often those other types of waste are found in things like the costs of supplies or extra workflow steps that reduce your daily capacity.

Unlike a bit of slack in staffing, these types of waste add no potential value to your bottom line. There's no benefit to patients when you pay more than you need to for consumables, or if your vaccine ordering routines lead to occasional expirations. This is pure waste with no potential upside.

And what are your best weapons for finding and eliminating these types of waste? Employees, aided by technology. They're your 'boots on the ground' in detecting waste that can be reduced for immediate profit improvement. They can notice other ways to improve processes, too. Aiming to cut staff to the point that they're always fully occupied with workflow tasks makes it hard, if not impossible, for staff to contribute in these more meaningful ways.

Bringing service back

Many of the most exciting front office technology tools don't just automate tasks; they allow patients to interact with your practice in the way they prefer. But it takes a while for patients to learn how to access and use these tools.

Having enough staff on hand to help patients scale the learning curve is another way to get the most from your technology investment. And, at the same time, your staff can reconnect with what probably drew them to medical office work in the first place: a desire to help patients. That personal touch—deemphasized in so many hectic practices in recent years—can make all the difference in retaining patients and attracting referrals.

Replacing an expense or increasing productivity?

When technology makes a practice more productive, it's often possible to interpret that extra productivity in two different ways. Has the technology replaced staff effort? Or is the technology allowing staff to do their jobs better?

If you've read this far, I'm sure you can guess which of these I think you should look at first. More productivity, more revenue, more profit: doesn't that have a nice ring to it?

The next case study takes a look at an experience I had working with a practice that solved some big problems with technology—and then saw how it opened a door to even bigger gains with people and technology working together.

CASE STUDY: Technology frees up staff time. Now what?

Executive Care is a seven-clinician primary practice I worked with a couple of years back that had workflow and profitability challenges. One pressing workflow problem was a constant back-up at reception. I believed that the causes of the bottleneck—collection efforts, new patient registration forms, past-due balances, etc.—were crying out for a technology solution.

I urged the owners and their recently hired administrator, Gary, to try a tablet check-in system that integrated with their EHR and PMS. Happily, the solution was a perfect fit. It enabled them to immediately improve their collection rate (an urgent need). And it helped staff avoid awkward collection conversations and time-consuming payment calculations at the front desk.

Hooray! right? Well, not so fast in this case. Gary and the practice owners thought they spotted a problem.

The two employees at the front desk who'd been so frantic and over-taxed suddenly had a lot less to do. They even had occasional idle time now. Gary and the physicians wondered if they should think about downsizing—maybe not right away, but through attrition over time.

But Gary, the owners, and I took a closer look and realized overstaffing was not actually a problem. Instead, we saw an opportunity to get the practice on a more solid financial footing—and forge new paths to growth.

"Extras" that were once essentials

Like so many practices my partners and I work with, this primary care practice had gradually paid less attention to many valuable front desk activities in recent years. Paperwork and collection chores had crowded out "niceties" like tidying the reception area throughout the day, communicating with the back office to troubleshoot delays, and supporting patients who were nervous or feeling very ill.

These cutbacks had been very costly to this particular practice—although they didn't fully realize it at the time, because staff felt so overwhelmed, and because the changes occurred gradually over time.

In addition to providing primary care, the practice was famed for its expertise managing a chronic, sometimes debilitating illness. The physicians were also well-known for managing several related conditions that patients could live with, but that required very careful management. This expertise was what had attracted more than a third of their patients.

The practice was also located in a wealthy area, where consumers expected top-shelf service. But the increasing burden of front desk duties, especially collections, had chipped away at the patient experience. There were longer waits at and after check-in, the reception area was frequently unkempt, and employees were sometimes too busy to offer their warmest welcome. This evolution was slowly causing attrition among their patients. But because there had been a reliable stream of newly diagnosed patients, the owners didn't perceive the churn. Plus, there were workflow problems that made everyone feel overworked, masking the extent of the exodus.

Our analysis exposed that nearly 35% of the practice's longstanding patients had left in the past few years and found new doctors, unbeknownst to the overtaxed team. The practice was benefiting from ever-greater numbers of new patients needing their expertise, but incurring costs from the exits of existing ones. Patients were starting to voice their aggravation on physician rating sites, too—another threat to profitability that was just starting to germinate.

Tablets bring relief

The tablets relieved the receptionists of some of their most frustrating tasks. Because the tablets could connect to health plans for payment information, they took the stress out of payment conversations. Patients understood—in many cases, for the first time—that their health plans determined their payment obligations, not the practice. Collections and payment compliance immediately went up. The receptionists were much less stressed, and now even had some free time on their hands.

Gary, the owners, and I realized that the practice now had an opportunity to redesign, even modernize, the receptionists' roles; they could take on new tasks the practice wasn't currently doing. Perhaps best of all, they could restore some of the "human touch" that had been lost when they became so focused on collections and paperwork.

Engaging the team

Gary met with the receptionists to brainstorm ideas. They were excited by the opportunity to elevate service and learn new skills. Gary was delighted by their energy, their commitment to the practice, and their excellent ideas for improving service.

The team suggested a few initiatives that could be implemented immediately. The reception area would be tidied hourly, and magazines replaced when they started looking worn. One receptionist suggested a water cooler and single-cup coffee brewer be installed. The pods could be stored at reception for patients to request, to keep costs down and encourage friendly interaction.

The receptionists also identified three important services had been getting less attention than they deserved:

1. Branded vitamins and supplements. The practice had a line of vitamins and supplements that was designed and overseen by the physicians. The reception team was supposed to offer and explain them as appropriate, but there had rarely been time. Some of these supplements were recommended by the physicians for patients depleted by their treatments, but the patients often didn't realize they could buy them on the way out. Patients would now receive more information about the products at check out.

2. The patient portal. The owners and the previous administrator had not urged the receptionists to promote the portal. Although patients asked about it, and the receptionists had been excited to help them use it at first, the learning curve had been steep. With so many other things to do at the front desk, there just wasn't time to help patients and their families get started with access before they left the office. Now there was enough flexibility at the front desk for one of the two receptionists to help new portal users get comfortable with the system during check-out.

3. Clinical trials. The practice had an extensive clinical research operation. The physicians thought that some patients who could benefit from a trial were intimidated or confused by the process. Now when patients had questions, the receptionists could encourage them to meet with a research coordinator while at the office.

Stewards of the patient experience

The receptionists began to see themselves as primarily responsible for the patient experience at the practice. They committed to making sure every patient left their visit feeling as cared for by the front office as by their physicians.

One suggested that they could offer new patients a brief tour of the facility, to help them feel welcome and appreciated. They would also make sure that patients knew about some of the more special features of the practice, like its after-hours emergency call service and weekend flu shot and nutritionist clinics.

In addition, the receptionists would keep a closer eye out for patients who'd been waiting a long time for their visit. The receptionists could intervene with a 'rescue'—either working with the back office to solve the bottleneck, or helping the patient reschedule if the wait would be too long. Patients would know that they weren't forgotten or ignored.

What else can technology—and staff—do now?

The tablets freed up receptionist capacity—and also unleashed their creativity and passion for service. Almost immediately, the practice was on a healthier footing, with better collections and happier patients. Positive reviews slowly started showing up online. Not surprisingly, Gary was excited to see where else in the practice technology and motivated staff could make magic together.

I recommended that Gary get in touch with the practice's PMS and EHR vendor. Many of our clients have found that their systems offer excellent features they weren't aware of.

Gary learned that there were several excellent, easily deployed features available that they weren't using:

- Patient payment portal
- Email statements
- Text appointment reminders
- Waiting lists
- Real-time eligibility checking

These solutions were quickly implemented, and now the scheduling and billing teams also had more time on their hands, even as they were able to do a better job verifying insurance and collecting.

Billers and schedulers up their service game

The "new" features of the PMS helped the billers and schedulers do a better job and work faster. Offering patients online bill pay and on-demand statements via email helped the billing and collections team save time. And online eligibility checking, in particular, helped the schedulers do a better job. The schedulers had been spending a lot of time checking and rechecking eligibility, often using payer portals. Now that they could do it right alongside scheduling—and they felt more confident in the information they gave patients. This helped patients better understand their financial responsibility before arriving for their visits.

Gary decided to let these teams come up with more ideas for improving their areas, just like the receptionists had.

The billers suggested that one of the team could now be trained up as a financial coordinator for the practice. She would work with patients who were facing more expensive therapies, to help them plan ahead for their deductible costs.

Some of the time the schedulers saved would be reinvested in their calls as they provided more detail about health plans' financial rules. This would continue to improve payment compliance.

The schedulers also had a couple of excellent ideas to enhance service. They had previously been keeping a paper waiting list for same-day appointments, but rarely got a chance to call patients to fill cancellations. Doing so would make patients happy and bring in more revenue. The new waiting list tool within the PMS would make the process much easier, so they'd be much more likely to use it.

The schedulers also had heard from many patients that the practice was not listed in the directories of health plans the practice accepted. They realized that it was an inconvenience for patients to call and check to see if the practice was actually in-network. Some prospective patients probably wouldn't bother—so the practice was unintentionally turning those patients away. Gary and the team decided that each scheduler could take responsibility for a subset of the plans they accepted, and make sure the practice was listed properly.

Tech liaisons

Gary recognized that the practice had left huge efficiency gains—and profit—on the table by not keeping up with the rollout of PMS and EHR features. To make sure that didn't happen again, he named a tech liaison for each system.

These were great opportunities for motivated staff to try something new and to feel they were contributing more to the practice. There were already two "power-users" that everyone informally relied on when they had questions. Now they would get credit for these contributions. They would also build career skills by working directly with vendors. Gary would also get help monitoring the frequent mail and training seminar opportunities the PMS/EHR vendor sent the practice's way.

Replacing and retaining patients: recalls and marketing

The creativity of the scheduling team, and the excellent new features of the PMS, got Gary thinking about other marketing efforts.

Once the payer directories were fixed, the team would start working on reviews and ratings directories, to make sure the practice could be discovered easily online. Gary first assigned the most important reviews and ratings directories to staff. The "owner" of a particular directory would be responsible for validating the information listed, claiming control of the practice's listings, and taking advantage of opportunities to enhance the listings. (We'll dig into the relatively simple yet powerful ideas behind managing online listings in Part Four.)

Gary also learned that a new vendor had created an online scheduling and reputation management tool that integrated with the practice's PMS. The software made it easy for patients to schedule via a computer or smartphone, providing their email and text information for confirmation.

He believed the practice's high-end patient base would welcome the flexibility to schedule online. The software and booking process also made it easy for staff to connect with the patient after their visit and request feedback or a review.

Gary wanted to ensure all the reviews sites got some attention, while also equally distributing the workload. He assigned each day of the week to a different staff member, who would follow up with those patients in the next few days after their visit. Each week, the entire team would focus on a particular directory, requesting that patients leave their reviews there.

Besides enhancing the practice's online reputation, Gary wanted to strengthen patient relationships with better outreach. Patients had not been recalled for annual preventive exams for many years, even though many had battled serious illnesses and could benefit from more proactive attention to their health. Moreover, many of the practice's patients were still dealing with chronic conditions and needed regular follow-up visits. Analyzing visit data using the EHR, Gary found that many of these patients were skipping follow-ups or falling behind on them.

Gary learned how to automate some of the steps to target patients for recalls using queries and custom reporting. Over time, they could use the portal and email to reach out to most patients for recalls. But in the short term, as the reception team worked towards training patients up on the portal, schedulers could reach out to patients by phone to schedule overdue visits.

The phone calls were initially discouraging, because they revealed that many patients had moved on to other doctors. But the calls did allow the schedulers to update the EHR with this information—cleaning up the records and giving Gary and the owners an accurate view of the number of patients the practice actually still had. This also allowed them to set goals for new patients in the next one to five years.

Gary was also now able to set a strategy for preventive visit scheduling. Like many practices, Executive Care experienced a drop-off in revenue in the first quarter of the year. Many patients were reluctant to get care after the holidays, when they faced both holiday credit card bills and fresh health plan deductibles. Gary worked with the schedulers to strategically book preventive visits during those first few months. Most patients could be seen for a preventive visit without paying a copay or deductible. The practice could expect to be paid reliably for these visits, and patients would not have to worry about the cost of care for the most part.

Looking ahead, Gary wanted to initiate other marketing projects that could be done in house. For example, he wanted to create newsletters for patients (to boost retention and engagement) and communication programs for referral partners. As the practice continued to take advantage of technology over the next few years, more staff time would be freed up to work on these goals. To prepare, Gary planned to create a comprehensive, three-to-five-year marketing plan for the practice in the coming months.

Planning for higher productivity

Gary was putting all the pieces in place for higher patient volume: better scheduling, effective reminders, additional marketing. And with patients using the tablets to complete their own history and chief complaint information, the back office MAs could handle more patients.

Gary and the physician team were all looking forward to higher productivity in the coming months. Everyone had the potential to earn more money and feel more productive. But with more marketing and fewer no-shows, would the MA team eventually need to be expanded?

Gary decided to proactively cross-train a floater/expediter from reception, and one from scheduling, who could help out in peak times. He also thought about potentially making a key addition to staff: an RN/case manager who could lead some larger clinical initiatives that he and the practice's owners had been discussing. This was quite a turnaround from our starting point, when they were contemplating cutting staff!

Thinking bigger: PCMH, CCM, group visits and more

One of the practice owners had a stack of articles about new care/reimbursement models that he thought the practice should explore. The stack had been gathering a lot of dust. The previous administrator had always put the ideas off. She argued that the practice was too strapped, and trying new approaches like the patient-centered medical home (PCMH) and Medicare's chronic care management (CCM) reimbursement opportunity would require more staff, which they couldn't afford. The physician was delighted that Gary and the team had been able to elevate the practice's productivity. Now the practice's better utilization of both technology and human talent opened the door to try some of these new models.

Gary first wanted to try establishing a group visit program. He thought this would be an easy first "win" for the practice. One of the owners was a charismatic, outgoing physician who would enjoy working with a group of patients at once. The practice's large number of patients managing chronic illness meant that there were natural groups to be formed. And the group visit model, unlike CCM and PCMH, wouldn't require additional skills or credentials beyond what the back office MA team currently held. Mainly, building the group visit program would be a matter of reaching out to the right patients systematically. This was something Gary was feeling much more confident about being able to do, with the practice's expanded use of its technology tools.

After starting monthly group visits, Gary decided that he and the billing team would work together on a plan for CCM. Gary investigated how some of the practice's MAs could become certified under the supervision of the physician team. This would enable the MAs to help with the monthly patient phone interactions required under CCM—allowing the MAs to generate new revenue for the practice. The MAs were excited at the prospect of adding to their own credentials and experience. The plan would start slowly, to give everyone the chance to scale the learning curve, and continue to provide excellent service.

Once these two programs were launched, the practice planned to bring on an RN to help expand the CCM effort, lead the PCMH certification process, and to help with other ideas the practice wanted to explore: telemedicine, expanded evening hours, and urgent care in the office.

Can you turn slack into profit? Some questions to ask

In the Executive Care project, the administrator, Gary, determined that the practice's new-found capacity was an opportunity to reinvest. Retaining the "extra" staff, but redirecting their efforts, had the potential to improve profit much more than downsizing.

Gary knew that demand for his practice's services was strong. And other metrics suggested that the current physician team had the potential to be more productive, if they had the right support. Greater productivity would yield higher profitability. Gary needed to figure out if—and how—the staff's roles could be reshaped to help make greater productivity possible.

Gary and I talked through how to consider the problem. We identified several key questions that helped him spot ways the practice could build long-term profitability by using staff differently, instead of taking a short-term gain by letting them go. These questions can help any practice think about more profitable ways to use staff talent:

1) *What worthwhile activities have slipped away as collection duties have mounted?*

The front desk of virtually every practice that takes insurance has been transformed in recent years. Collection activities have, by necessity, surged to the top of the priority list. As collecting has become more important, the patient experience in many practices has changed. Many patients would say it has not changed for the better.

Technology can help front desk staff reclaim some of the time they've spent estimating amounts due and collecting. That presents an opportunity to enhance service at the front desk. How can your practice make use of it? What would make patients remember their experience at your practice in a positive way, starting with checking in at the front desk?

2) *What essentials have been done poorly, put off, or done infrequently because employees are always at capacity?*

If your practice has long been committed to keeping headcount as low as possible, it's likely some activities that could make your practice more profitable are not being done, or are not being done consistently. Answering this question requires a long, honest look at consistency throughout your workflow. For example, are email and cell contacts collected every time a patient schedules? Is insurance verified every time? In the back office, are rooms always tidied promptly between uses?

Tasks that are important but not urgent, such as managing payer directories, deploying new technology, or recalling patients for follow-up or preventive care are likely to slip down the to-do list when everyone feels rushed. Can you estimate the profit foregone by not doing these things?

3) What ideas do employees have for improving service and maintaining quality?

It's appropriate to see waste as the enemy of profitability. But it's hard to spot it and correct it on your own. You need eyes and ears at each point in your workflow to see what's really happening. That's another pitfall of keeping staff so lean that employees are maxed out: it leaves little opportunity to spot and make improvements. Employees can often be first to spot waste that adds no value whatsoever, things like paying too much for supplies or ordering magazines no one reads.

Employees are often the best source of ideas your practice could ask for. In our consulting work at Capko & Morgan, we are always impressed by the attention staff pays to details and the great ideas employees have for improving patient service and workflow. But it's not common for them to be asked to share those ideas. Practices that don't encourage employees to suggest improvements and help troubleshoot problems are underutilizing some of their best assets.

4) Are physicians and NPPs doing tasks that staff could do?

Keeping everyone focused on work at the top of their skills and credentials helps your practice gets the most productivity out of all its resources. When physicians do work that a manager, nurse, or MA could do, that's time they're not spending seeing patients. Physicians, NPs, PAs, and other clinicians all want to spend as much of their time as possible doing what they're trained to do. And that's what brings in the money! Finding and eliminating distractions from their primary responsibilities can increase your clinicians' productive capacity. And they'll be happier, too.

It's not always easy to find small leaks of physician and NPP time. You'll need to carefully observe your workflow, shadowing your physicians. But it will be time and effort well-invested if you can find, and eliminate, ways that physician time is being siphoned off on tasks others can do.

5) *What 'big ideas' or new opportunities have we not considered because everyone has been too busy?*

This one may be easy to answer. Do you have a stack of articles and newsletters on your desk (or bookmarked in a browser) about new programs and initiatives that might work for your practice, "if only we had the resources"?

If technology makes your staff more productive, that newfound capacity might be the starting point for reconfiguring staff jobs to support new initiatives. But what if that's still not enough?

Practices often hold back from considering new programs simply because they might have to hire another staff member or two. But what if the revenue potential greatly exceeds the cost of adding the needed support? If you've internalized "rules" about always minimizing staff, those assumptions may hold you back from trying out programs that could put your practice on a more profitable trajectory. Building a workflow to support CCM or pursuing PCMH certification can also be energizing for physicians, and these programs elevate the practice's image with patients, too.

With more nurses and MAs interested in working part-time, per diem, or on a temporary basis, it's easier than ever to add staff slowly. This can be useful for building towards a program like CCM—or simply for gauging whether a bit more staff can help your practice reach a higher level of productivity and profitability.

When overstaffing is real

By now I hope I've made it clear that, in my experience, understaffing is more common than overstaffing in medical practices. And it can be a lot more costly, too—especially for independent practices. That's why I believe it's so important not to miss opportunities to be more profitable by having a bit more staff, or to cause avoidable losses by going too lean. Employees are not just a practice *expense,* they're an *investment*—assets that can drive more profit.

Of course, there are some situations in which overstaffing is more likely. When you make a decision to outsource an entire function, e.g., your billing, it may not be easy to plug those employees into different roles in the practice. (And in a case like billing, with its specialized expertise, the employees may not want to do something different.)

We've worked with practices that have seen physicians retire, and haven't wanted to trim staff, even though they haven't replaced the physicians. But even in those cases, it's possible that the employees could be put to use doing work that generates a profit—and keeping them on board may provide needed slack. It depends on whether there is productive work that is not being done.

By far the most common scenario of overstaffing we see involves physicians and NPPs who are well-supported, but still not seeing as many patients as they could or would like to. In these cases, assuming local demand is strong, the problem is usually marketing. When physicians are new to a market, it takes time to build up a base of patients. MAs hired to support a new physician may be able to help with marketing tasks while volume is lower.

Sometimes, vague production targets and inefficient scheduling contribute to suppressed physician productivity. Adjusting them, while providing enough support, can help ensure everyone on the team hits their stride.

When physicians start their first jobs after clinical training, they start on a new learning curve in practice. Reaching the productivity level of an experienced physician can be daunting. Mentoring from more experienced physicians is essential. Experienced staff can help, too. Typically, new physicians wind up with new nurse or MA support. But that can mean that the entire team has to learn how to be productive in a new practice. Although more experienced doctors may be reluctant to part with their seasoned staff, sharing them, even temporarily, can help newer physicians get up to speed more quickly.

And what if demand for your service is weak in your area? Thankfully, this is relatively rare in medicine. But if you're unlucky enough that demand in your area is too weak to grow your practice at all, adding more staff may not help you increase your volume—and being properly staffed will still help you be more efficient and use your time optimally. For example, if you're a solo physician and the volume your practice currently generates can be served in three days, can you see patients elsewhere another day or half day in an adjacent market? The right staff can help you optimize your schedule—and keep your patient flow efficient, and patients well-served, on the days you're in your office.

Optimizing is an ongoing goal

Recognizing that optimal staffing is more than just "getting by" with the fewest staff possible is just part of the battle. Having enough staff is the first step—but then you have to use them in the right ways. Skilled, experienced, dedicated staff can be an invaluable asset to your practice. But getting the most from their efforts—and keeping them engaged and dedicated—requires attention to the content of their jobs. As technology enables employees to be more productive and do their work better, opportunities emerge for employees to add more value.

The best clues to understaffing also provide road signs to new ways employees can elevate your practice. Take a look at these areas. If your practice can do better, perhaps more staff can help. Or perhaps it's time for a review of job structure, and an exploration of how new technology can help your staff do more.

 - *Physician productivity* - How do your physicians measure up in terms of number of patients, weekly visits, gross charges, and procedures? Are physicians routinely "helping out" with tasks others could do? Are doctors and NPPs often waiting for patients?

 - *Overtime* - Is your practice relying on overtime to meet routine needs?

- *Patient service* - How satisfied are patients with their interactions with staff in scheduling, check-in, and billing? Are wait times tolerable? Do patients engage with staff? Is scheduling providing adequate access, including urgent appointments and access to a functioning waiting list? Are patients being recalled as appropriate for care?

- *Errors and delays (conformance quality)* - Does rushing in one part of the workflow lead to errors down the line? (For example, are billers doing extra work—and losing revenue—because some details are sometimes missed in scheduling or at the front desk?) Are calls answered promptly, or are they often abandoned? Does work have to be redone because key information is misplaced or not properly entered into systems? Is the practice exceeding benchmarks on billing metrics, or are collection tasks delayed?

- *Flexibility* - Can your practice deal with sudden surges or absences without undue stress or compromising patient service?

- *Marketing and reputation management* - Are staff monitoring, correcting, and polishing online listings with payers and reviews directories? Does your practice offer regular "TLC" to its referral partners?

- *Missed/delayed opportunities* - Can your practice consider new payer programs or clinical initiatives, or is staff capacity always a concern? Are managing partners and managers/administrators too busy to do strategic analyses of new opportunities?

 - *Missed improvements* - Are staff empowered and encouraged to spot waste and inefficiency? Are they able to make suggestions to improve the practice's efficiency and service? Are you able to keep up with technology improvements that could make your practice more efficient?

- *Training/learning* - Are management and staff encouraged to learn and build skills, not just clinicians? Are there avenues for staff to add skills that can help the practice, such as new certifications?

PART TWO

Workflow Hacks: Quick Tips to Think Like a Consultant

One of the biggest advantages of hiring consultants like my group, Capko & Morgan, to assess your practice's performance is that we can take a holistic view at your operations. It's hard to do that on your own. Whether you are a busy physician or busy manager, you're, you know, busy. The day-to-day demands of your practice make it difficult to stop what you're doing and watch. Plus, it's challenging to be objective about processes you established in the first place—and to compare your practice to others when, of course, you work in just one. But that doesn't mean you couldn't—with the right information and mindset—take a closer look at your workflow, and make some of the same observations a consultant would. This section of the book cherry-picks a few of my favorite workflow signposts and opportunities, to help you get started.

When a consultant walks into your practice, she instinctively looks for signs that your workflow could be made more efficient. We really can't help but notice these things: it's as if it's in our blood. But you can start to think like us, even if you'll never find yourself obsessing about workflow as you butter your toast in the morning.[13]

Here are a few of the principles we keep in mind and common signs of inefficiency we look for while walking your halls.

Jumping beans, multitasking, and other false economies

One of the first things we'll notice after arriving at your practice is whether your receptionists are in constant motion: constantly popping up from their chairs like jumping beans to go scan insurance cards or documents, for example, or use other frequently accessed equipment like printers, fax machines and credit card swipers.

If employees need to use a particular machine over and over again, speed up your workflow by putting one right next to them. Or, better yet, look into whether innovation has made a better/smaller/cheaper option available.

For example, many practice management systems are compatible with small-footprint insurance card readers that take up very little room on a desk. These little devices don't just eliminate the back-and-forth between the reception desk and the scanner. They usually also transfer data from the card right into the patient's record, eliminating the need for key information to be manually typed in by staff. That also means fewer errors that could create more work down the road in billing, when claims are rejected or denied. That's a lot of value from a little device that you can probably obtain for less than $100.

---

[13] Alas, I have done this. For proof of my obsession with process efficiency, see "Toast, workflow, and the quest for productivity" at www.capko.com/toast-and-workflow. My partners are equally intrigued by workflow ideas.

Small monitors are another common time-waster. If employees have to scroll through multiple screens to get to information that's needed every time they schedule or check a patient in, larger monitors (or multiple monitors) can speed up those transactions significantly. That translates to happier patients, more transactions completed per employee, and maybe even less overtime over the course of a year.

Sometimes, clients tell us they are aware that these additions will make work faster and easier, but the purchases are delayed to save money. But these "savings" are a false economy—despite frugal intentions, these decisions likely cost more over time. The cash outlay for these additions can be quickly recouped in greater efficiency, especially since the cost of all sorts of computer hardware has dropped in recent years. We also sometimes hear from clients that they're reluctant to spend money helping staff be more efficient, because more efficiency will just mean idle time. But what if everyone's always fully loaded or even overloaded because you're *not* maximizing efficiency? That likely means you don't have the resources for important-but-not-urgent tasks—so they don't get done. You also may find that a small increase in load causes bigger problems than it should, because no one has capacity to spare.

Improve office efficiency, and you decrease the odds that patients will be kept waiting while an employee completes clerical tasks that have no perceived value to patients at all. How much happier will your patients be if what they remember is spending time with you—not waiting in a check-in line, or on hold on the phone trying to make an appointment? What could that mean for your practice in terms of referrals and positive reviews? Heck, an efficient, pleasant experience with the administrative side of your practice might even make your patients more likely to pay their bills promptly. And as you increase efficiency, you even may be able to see more patients.

Multitasking: doing more tasks less quickly

Multitasking is a pernicious productivity drainer. It seems like you're doing two things at once, but you're really switching back and forth between the tasks. And each time you switch, it takes a moment or two for your brain to refocus. Over the course of a day, this can add up to a whole lot of lost productivity.[14]

Physicians and managers who set aside closed-door time to concentrate on, say, completing a backlog of charts or working on a budget reforecast have already figured this out for themselves: Doing a complex task well requires focus. So why would it be different for staff?

The most common task we see combined with other jobs in practices is answering the phone. But dedicated phone/scheduling staff is by far the most efficient approach for most practices. When employees try to handle phone calls while, say, checking patients in, neither task gets full attention. (So which patient are you comfortable letting down?) When phone calls are juggled with other tasks, more mistakes will happen. Errors in scheduling, for example, could impact your ability to get paid down the road. These costs can be much higher than the "savings" of having employees do two things at once.

Multitasking is stressful for employees, too—and that impacts morale, potentially leading to turnover. The patient experience will also suffer when employees are stressed out. The costs of this are not immediately obvious, but they can be significant over time.

---

[14]As much as 40% of productivity is lost, according to some experts. See this article from the American Psychological Association:
http://www.apa.org/research/action/multitask.aspx

Lumpy scheduling, missed batching

In some practices, patients need to have brief visits for blood draws, injections, or other quick checks or services handled by MAs or nurses. Because these tasks are so quick to complete, it can be tempting to offer this subset of patients the option to come in at any time of the day. But this may result in an MA being interrupted in the middle of a busy morning or afternoon to help a single patient, breaking up her day and process flow. Other days may be even more inefficiently booked, with many patients coming in at random times.

Usually, there are blocks of time that are convenient for almost all patients. Selecting such a block of time for booking these services—say, 3:00-5:00—will allow nearly everyone to be served conveniently, while also allowing your nurse or MA to be more productive the rest of the day. (If a few patients can't come in during the block, just those few patients could be handled as exceptions.) Over time, scheduling can be optimized so that only the number of blocks that are needed are reserved for these services—and they can even be offered on a walk-in basis in some cases, reducing scheduling overhead.

Similarly, lumpy physician scheduling can also result from being unnecessarily flexible. When patients call in to book, staff may be inclined to ask, "When would you like to come in?" instead of offering slots that allow the practice to be more productive. But patients may be indifferent to the flexibility—meaning that the practice incurs a cost without the patient receiving a tangible benefit.

Extraneous actions and valueless tasks

Here's a quick way to recapture value: eliminate valueless work. When staff is busy doing work that doesn't produce anything, then there's less time available for work that does.

Here are a few examples that you might find in your own practice—or that may help you think about where else wasted effort could be lurking.

Extraneous actions

One of the most common forms of wasted effort we look for in practices is extra steps in the rooming process. For example, an MA might be tasked with retrieving patients, then bringing them to a station for weight and vitals checking. The MA waits a moment while the patient finds a place for her purse, takes off her shoes, steps on the scale. Once the vitals are checked, the patient puts her shoes back on and collects her belongings, while the MA waits to lead the next leg of their little tour of the office. Best case: the MA will now escort the patient to an exam room. Worst case: the MA escorts the patient back to reception for more waiting—maximizing the number of steps and delays the MA will incur to complete what should be a direct trip to the exam room.

The detour to the vitals station feels like progress, but adds steps that take time and benefit no one. It takes noticeably longer to check vitals and weight this way than it would in the exam room. Scales and blood pressure cuffs are cheap compared to the time wasted with these extra steps over weeks, months, and years. Plus, the vitals station usually becomes a bottleneck (more on this later), reducing productivity. And when MAs are constantly in motion, taking steps that aren't helping to move the patient through the workflow, it's harder to gauge how much capacity your practice actually has.

Lots of effort, little or no value

Another common waste of staff resources is sorting faxes or voicemails that could be pre-sorted with automation. When faxes are received on paper, they must be collected, sorted, and delivered by a human. That's a lot of work (not to mention paper and toner) that could be avoided with electronic faxes. And beyond just receiving the faxes electronically, they can be pre-sorted fairly accurately simply by using different numbers for referrals, billing, pharmacy, lab, etc. This type of "automation" can save precious time and reduce the risk of an important fax being misplaced, and it costs only as much as an additional phone number.

Voicemails that arrive in a general mailbox similarly create unnecessary work. Patients will happily direct themselves to the person who can help them if they're given access to a user-friendly phone tree. Making sure that enough staff is available to answer phones, and that they're properly trained to handle the calls they receive, helps ensure that messages don't pile up. This can save time and money over the long term, because responding to voicemails adds steps and takes much longer, on average, than handling a call as it comes in. Leaving a message and waiting to reconnect is more inconvenient for patients, too—and prospective patients may decline to leave a message, and call your competition instead.

Opening mail is another easily minimized time-waster. Switch to electronic funds transfer (EFT) for all payers, and you'll not only get rid of a wasteful manual task, you'll get your money in the bank right away, without a trip there. And your PMS will probably accept electronic transmissions of remittance advices and EOBs once you flip the switch on EFT—cutting out more manual labor. Use your bank's lockbox service for patient check—and give patients a payment portal so more of them will pay online.

Manually creating and mailing checks for accounts payable is another labor-intensive task that can be easily streamlined with online banking. Some banks even offer varied levels of access so that the practice administrator or bookkeeper could set up payments that won't be transmitted until approved by the account owner.

Reducing steps and handling of checks and other documents saves time and money. And it also reduces the chance of an item going missing—thereby creating more work to track it down.

Another typical valueless task we look for is collecting—or rather, attempting to collect—old debt by calling patients. Calling to collect debt that has been outstanding for months or even years is unlikely to generate enough income to cover collection costs. Instead, develop a clear policy for handling past-due accounts and sending them to a professional collection agency once they pass the final deadline.

Obsolescence happens

As technology improves, tasks that were once essential can lose value. What's more, many of today's technology advances will ultimately be transitional, replaced in the future by even more efficient ways to do the same work. This is why it's so important to continually evaluate and improve your workflow. Optimizing is never done. Think of it as a lifetime journey of improvement, not a single destination.

Bottlenecks and the relative value of resources

Bottlenecks are the points in a process where production slows or stops, because a downstream step in the process can't begin until an earlier step finishes. Patient flow within a practice is typically a very dependent process. The steps are completed in a specific order, and later steps can't begin until the ones before them finish. For example, patients can't be seen until they're checked in, and their vitals and reasons for seeing the doctor are recorded. When any step backs up and becomes a bottleneck, the entire process slows down.

Finding a bottleneck in your patient flow is relatively straightforward, once you start looking. Just look for who is waiting and where they're waiting—and then figure out why.

The complete flow of a patient through the practice will be limited by the slowest process—the process that is holding everything back. Figure out what's slowing the throughput down, and you may be able to speed the flow up and add productivity if you can improve that slowest component.

For example, if patients are waiting in a long line at reception, there's a bottleneck there. If MAs and physicians are also waiting because of this bottleneck, then their productivity is restricted. Adding more resources at the front desk to clear the bottleneck will reduce unproductive physician time—a good thing. Even one more patient seen per day could mean more than enough revenue to fund an additional receptionist role—plus, that person could do more tasks than simply speeding up check-in. (Better still, you might be able to increase front desk through-put with technology, such as tablets or kiosks to allow patients to check themselves in.)

And what if there's no line at reception, but patients are cooling their heels in the lounge, while physicians are also waiting for their patients to be roomed? Perhaps you have too few MAs. (Another sign: are physicians sometimes rooming their own patients?) Or are MAs waiting their turn at your scale/vitals station? Put scales and vitals equipment in your rooms, and immediately speed up throughput. MAs not only won't need to wait for a scale, they also won't have to look up the patient's record more than once, or wait while the patient picks up their belongings and shoes. (Patients will value the privacy when getting weighed, too.)

If MAs and physicians alike are waiting for a room to become available, perhaps you have too few rooms—or perhaps they're being used for things that could be done elsewhere, such as phlebotomy. Or perhaps rooms have been set aside for specific doctors—without fully factoring in the variability each physician's potential volume.

Highest and best uses of resources

Some delays in workflow are more costly than others. If you have a bottleneck or constraint in your workflow that causes physicians to wait when they're ready to see a patient, that's a bottleneck you must correct to improve clinician productivity.

Physicians are the moneymakers for your practice. They're the only people who can do the work that they do. And they're also your most expensive resources. You need to have enough resources supporting your doctors and NPPs so that they're not idle when they want to be busy, and they're not doing work that a staff member could do at lower cost.

Rooms are another very valuable resource, sometimes a scarce one in practices. Just like your physicians, you want to keep them busy serving their most productive purpose: hosting patient visits with clinicians. If physicians are waiting for rooms that are being used for lower-value purposes, that's a productivity loss to your practice.

And what if you have found you just don't have enough rooms to cure your waiting clinician problem? Well, then it's time to get creative. Could you adjust days off and practice hours to stretch room capacity? We often find that practices assume that none of their physicians, PAs, NPs or back office support would ever want to work an early or late schedule or a Saturday, but are surprised to find that's not true once they ask.

Sometimes, it's smart to put a remodel on the table. If your practice still has individual offices for your physicians, you might want to rethink this—especially if they're large. An office that shares a wall with an exam room can sometimes be converted fairly easily to an exam room, because plumbing is nearby. If adding exam room space can allow your doctors to earn more money and be less annoyed by idle time, that could easily take the sting out of sharing an office.

Smoothing the process

When physicians are stuck waiting for patients instead of seeing them, that's a deadweight loss of productivity and revenue. Fixing that should be a higher priority than other bottlenecks if your practice is aiming to boost the number of patients you're seeing.

But that doesn't mean that other wait times don't matter. Overbooking the schedule and cranking up the workflow at the front end so that patients end up waiting 20 or 30 minutes or more in exam rooms may ensure that your doctors aren't ever idle, but there might be other negative consequences when patients start to feel understandably peeved.

For example, you may find patients complain—either diverting staff attention to listen to them, or posting negative comments online. Perhaps some patients won't be able to wait, and will have to reschedule. Unhappy patients cause stress while they're in the office. And a large backlog of patients waiting can sometimes cause confusion about who should be seen first, delaying the process further.

Japanese management principles and Lean thinking teach smoothness as a process flow goal. Removing bottlenecks to help your clinicians be more productive is the right starting point, but also aim for a smooth process to help ensure stress and chaos don't undermine your efforts.

Data capture and scheduling

When we look for bottlenecks and analyze wait times in practices, we'll literally follow patients as they progress through each step of a practice's workflow, marking start and end times to calculate average waits. You might find this challenging—you'll likely need to set aside at least a few hours over several days. Alternatively, you may be able to get at this data much more easily if your EHR has timestamp features.

The big pitfall with timestamp data, though, is garbage in, garbage out. Your calculations will only be as good as your timestamp data—staff must be trained to enter it properly. Staying on top of these timestamps can be an annoyance for staff at first. Staff may initially resist if the importance of accurate data isn't clear. But when the data is properly captured, you'll have a very objective tool for analyzing wait times and refining workflow, enabling everyone to work more efficiently. You will also be able to see opportunities for tweaking your appointment slots to improve patient wait times and maybe even add capacity—both huge potential payoffs.

New technology is emerging that uses RFID badges to capture location data and automatically update practice systems. It is available for a growing number of EHR and PMS platforms, and may be a more appealing alternative to relying on manual data entry, especially as the price of RFID comes down over time.

Untapped software features that can make your practice more efficient

These days, it's rare for us to work with a practice that doesn't have both an EHR and a PMS in place. But what's rarer still is to find a practice that is actually using these systems to their fullest advantage.

It's common for vendors to update these systems very frequently, especially cloud-based systems. It can be a challenge to keep up with all the roll-outs, and to distinguish between upgrades that add important features versus ones that offer minor improvements. But not keeping up with them often means missed opportunities to improve workflow efficiency and even revenue capture. That's why we always check to see if all system features that could improve practice efficiency have been implemented.

Here are a few of the features that your practice might have overlooked that can help improve workflow immediately. These examples aren't exhaustive, though, and there undoubtedly will be more in the future. (We'll also explore others in Part Five.) Developing a system for staying in touch with vendors to make sure important upgrades are deployed can help you continually improve our workflow. And it could be an excellent career growth opportunity for a staff member who's interested in technology and cager to build skills.

Integration

An integrated EHR and PMS set-up enables automatic transfer of superbill information from the EHR to the billing system once a physician has signed off on his or her chart note. Because it eliminates the need to repeatedly re-enter data, using a PMS that's integrated with your EHR is one of the most reliable ways to reduce billing problems and save time. Yet many practices still use two separate systems that don't share data—so every day, staff enters the same data in multiple places, a huge amount of duplicate work that increases the probability of errors. These errors, in turn, slow down billing, and may even lead to rejected or denied claims.

Sometimes, we encounter practices that don't realize their current systems can be integrated.

For example, they might assume that they have to use a PMS from the same vendor as their EHR. If they don't like the PMS that their EHR vendor offers, they'll assume they're out of luck, without inquiring about other systems their EHR can integrate with. (These days, most EHRs will integrate at least partially with at least a few other vendors' PMSs.)

Occasionally, we even encounter a practice that is using EHR and PMS software from the same vendor, but the two haven't been set up to take full advantage of integration. For example, we worked with a practice recently that had been on the same (highly rated) EHR for more than 10 years, and added a PMS from the same vendor about five years later. Although the system was set up to pass demographic information from the PMS to the EHR, the superbill information from the chart was not being passed through. Because it had never worked as it should, the practice team just assumed that more integration wasn't possible. All it took was a few calls to the vendor to find out how to turn on the additional integration. This saved the practice's billing service hours of manual effort each week and sped up the claims cycle considerably.

Even when you're set on an EHR that isn't designed to integrate with any PMS you're comfortable using (or vice versa), third party solutions providers can often build a custom link between the systems you prefer. If you're processing many bills, the positive ROI on this investment can be significant—and quickly realized.

Workflow tracking

Integrated EHR/PMS systems typically offer electronic time-stamps to track patients' progress through their visit. Yet practices rarely seem to take full advantage of these tools. For example, we see practices using the "arrived" and "ready" stamps at the front desk to alert the back office when patients can be roomed, but then the back may use only the "in room" stamp, and not note when the physician arrives or when the patient exits the room. Without data for when the physician arrives and leaves, the length of the wait time and the length of the encounter can't be calculated.

Entering this data takes only a moment, but to busy nurses and MAs, it can seem like a tedious task with no payoff. When you start entering this data regularly and correctly, though, you gain a useful tool for analyzing workflow and identifying trouble spots. Everyone can benefit from this kind of analysis, especially the back office staff, which often bears the brunt of stress when patient wait times expand.

Overlooked cloud options

Cloud-based EHR/PMS options offer many advantages to practices—especially small and medium practices without in-house technology teams. One of the most important is that they lower the risk of downtime that can derail a day's productivity[15]. Cloud systems are usually automatically updated—meaning your practice can take advantage of work-saving features as soon as they're available, with no server upgrade needed.

Switching can be a very significant project if you're migrating between different vendors or even different systems from the same vendor. But cloud-based *versions* of many systems that once were only available server-based are becoming much more common. These options can give your practice the benefits of the cloud with fewer hassles than switching to a completely different platform.

Some practice managers and physicians are reluctant to consider the cloud because they're concerned about security. It's absolutely critical to discuss security protections with your vendor, to understand how they approach keeping your patient data safe, and to feel confident in how they're accepting that responsibility. But remember that a cloud vendor likely has a team focused on keeping the data of its many customers safe. Any server in your own office would be safeguarded only by people you hire, who likely won't be focusing solely on that task. Plus, your server will be only as se-

---

[15] You can lower it further still by making sure you have backup access to the internet in case of an outage. And always be sure to ask the vendor what work-arounds are recommended in the event of an internet outage.

cure as your office. Hacking is not the only risk to your data; theft is a risk as well (along with damage from fire or other catastrophe).

Electronic verification and authorization

In the past few years, most of the cloud-based PMS vendors (and some EHR vendors) have rolled out real-time eligibility checking, but it is often overlooked or not fully deployed by practices.

Real-time eligibility checking lets staff transmit patient data to health plans and receive near-immediate verification of coverage and terms. It's all done right from the patient's record—so staff doesn't waste time toggling screens. The patient's record will also be updated with the plan's response—no need to type a note. Many steps are eliminated, and the verification is more reliable, too. Batch checking, also commonly available, is a handy tool for re-checking eligibility for all patients a day or two ahead of their visit, eliminating dozens of steps.

Electronic prior authorizations, or ePA, is another relatively new tool that can significantly reduce processing time. Systems like Surescripts and CoverMyMeds are add-ons to most EHRs and PMSs. These tools cut out many prior authorization steps, and speed up the process significantly.

Sometimes we find practices have held back on using electronic verification and authorization because some of their contracted plans aren't using the systems, or aren't using them fully. But participation has increased over time, as has the quality and quantity of data transmitted (and that trend will likely continue). Even without perfect payer participation, there are benefits to using these tools for plans that have embraced them. Waiting for perfection often means missing out on efficiency gains today.

Waiting lists

Many practice management systems offer waiting lists, but we find they're rarely used. An automated waiting list allows staff to keep track of patients who want to come in sooner than they can be booked—when a cancellation occurs, it takes only a click or two to move the patient from the waiting list into the open spot. This can be an invaluable way to maintain an efficient schedule, while also upping service. And it's a lot faster than the old-fashioned, unreliable method of jotting notes onto paper lists.

Built-in reminders

Text and email reminders are built into most PMS and EHR systems. But often practices are unaware they already own this technology, and instead assume they'll have to work with another vendor—which often means automated reminders never get deployed.

Electronic reminders don't just free up staff time. Patients increasingly prefer electronic reminders to phone calls. These reminders also can be much more effective. Gen X and millennial patients, especially, tend to delete voicemails without listening to them, and to ignore calls from unfamiliar numbers. Text and email reminders are more likely to be acknowledged by these patients.

Is self-service working for you?

Besides making staff more efficient, technology has the potential to transform your workflow by transferring some of the workload to some very enthusiastic volunteers: your patients.

The growing consumer preference for self-service has been well-documented in other industries, but medicine has acted on it more slowly. Even if you're wary about technology because you've been let down in the past, this trend is one you should take a closer look at, because it offers a win-win for your practice and your patients.

Payment portals, for example, can significantly increase the likelihood that your practice will be paid promptly by patients. As patients' share of the cost of care continues to increase, so does the importance of encouraging payment compliance. One of the best ways to do that is to remove obstacles like the availability of a stamp or the need to call during business hours to pay by credit card. Plus, adding the ability to pay online and receive statements electronically cuts out a lot of handling—making your revenue cycle faster, more efficient, and more profitable.

Online scheduling presents another big opportunity to increase efficiency. Some PMS and EHR systems offer it, but for those that don't, third party companies have emerged recently that combine online scheduling with reputation management tools. These products integrate with most practice PMSs, capturing not just the appointment the patient booked, but also demographic info. And because they require patients to register, you're able to capture the patient's email without asking for it at the time of service–so you'll also be able to send electronic statements. You'll likely get paid faster, while also saving statement mailing costs.

The order of things

Tools like online scheduling and patient portals don't just shift some of the workload onto patients. They also allow for that work to be done at any time of day. Reconsidering the normal order of tasks in your practice can help you get more from your workflow. Sometimes, a more efficient or effective flow can come from changing up your conventions.

For example, over the past decade, copays and other patient payments have come to account for a much bigger chunk of practice revenue. But it took many practices a long time start collecting these amounts at the time of service. Those that made the shift more quickly and consistently were positioned to collect more effectively from patients. They have been less harmed by the trend towards higher copays and deductibles.

New technology that can help employees do tasks better also provides an opportunity to rethink how work is done in the medical office, in what order, and by whom.

For example, as better verification and estimation tools roll out, schedulers can do a better job of validating insurance information and preparing patients to pay—and they can do it in less time. Some of that saved time could be spent on tasks like signing patients up for portal account(s) before the first visit, instead of waiting until they're in the office. This can enable patients to supply registration information electronically, either at home or on a tablet in the office—either way, costs are saved because the information is more accurate and doesn't require manual entry.

Continue learning and experimenting

Technology is making tasks that used to be valuable less so—providing new opportunities to streamline workflow or even rejigger it for higher efficiency. Healthcare reform continues to alter the payment landscape. Even patient preferences are evolving in ways that will impact your practice's workflow.

Management is like medicine in that to do it really well, continuous learning is necessary. Physicians and managers who team up to continually work on practice operations have a significant advantage over those who rely on old assumptions or don't consider management a serious discipline.

Sometimes, as you break new ground with untested ideas for workflow improvement, you'll find it's hard for your practice to adapt at first. Changes to workflow can be challenging, and patience is essential. You may even occasionally find that, despite the most careful planning, one of your change initiatives just doesn't work out for your practice. Just remember that it's okay to try new things, even if they don't all work. After all, no improvement will come without change. What's important is to plan well before making changes, evaluate critically as you proceed, and be ready to make adjustments as needed.

Learning to spot workflow changes that will help, versus ones that may do more harm than good, is the subject we'll tackle next in Part Three, *Patient Flow Mistakes Smart Managers Make—and How to Avoid Them.*

PART THREE

Patient Flow Mistakes Smart Practice Managers Make—and How to Avoid Them

Savvy practice administrators and physicians know that there is gold locked up in patient flow. More efficient processes mean less waiting time, less aggravation (for you and your patients), more visits and procedures completed, and a stronger bottom line. It's no wonder that this is the first place many practices look to make management improvements—and that so many conferences, articles, and books offer to help them 'crack the code' of patient flow.

Yet despite all this attention, workflow problems remain one of the biggest challenges for practices. Implementing changes to workflow can sometimes be like walking a minefield. My colleagues and I have worked with practices around the country that have seen their process improvements yield no benefit whatsoever. Sometimes they even backfire and make process problems worse.

What is it that makes improving workflow so challenging, even for high-performing practices? One big stumbling block is that motivated managers and physicians act too quickly, aiming to solve whatever problems they think they see, instead of first identifying the most useful problem to solve.

It sounds easy, but determining the right problem to solve regularly trips up brilliant and experienced scientists, engineers, and managers in every industry—so much so that dozens of management books, articles and even academic papers have been written on the subject. Albert Einstein himself even reputedly quipped, "If I were given one hour to save the planet, I would spend 59 minutes defining the problem and one minute resolving it." So, don't feel bad if you've found that some of your own workflow solutions have failed to pan out. You're in pretty stellar company.

Finding the right problem to solve is difficult because the wrong ones look just as important. But there are techniques that can help you separate the problems that make a real difference from the red herrings—in this section, I'll pass along a few tricks I've learned that can help.

The (ironic) problem of glaring inefficiencies

Sharp-eyed and driven managers are naturally inclined to spot inefficiencies, and feel compelled to fix them as soon as they're spotted. (Really, who can resist fixing a process that's just taking way too long? It's like a gauntlet thrown right in your path.) Managers and physicians that have had a bit of operations management training, such as Lean training, tend to become even more attuned to waste and inefficiencies in the various steps of their practice flow.

Sometimes, though, the problem right in front of you is a distraction from real sources of inefficiency in your workflow. "Fixing" something that isn't truly broken can deplete resources available for more profitable or urgent tasks down the road. What's more, the processes in patient flow are usually highly interdependent—meaning that a change in one step may affect a later step. Changing a process in your workflow simply because it stands out as wasteful won't necessarily contribute to a smoother or faster overall cycle. It might even throw the flow further out of sync, making wait times longer.

CASE STUDY: The superstar psychiatric clinic

One of our most delightful recent clients was a psychiatric clinic that had grown dramatically and was providing critical services in its region. It was one of the only such resources available for many of its patients, who were extremely grateful and happy with the care they received.

The dynamic physician-owner of the practice consulted us to find ways to improve efficiency—and especially to improve profitability, which hadn't really kept pace with practice growth. One of the first places we looked for improvement was the front desk, because like most practices that accept insurance, the Superstar Psychiatric Clinic needed to collect a growing portion of its revenue from patients.

It didn't take us long to figure out that the clinic's front desk was doing an unusually poor job at collecting from patients. In fact, most of the time the staff just automatically said, "Don't worry, we'll bill you," and hustled patients along without even trying to collect copays or balances.

When we pointed the problem out to the office manager, she explained that it was just impossible to collect effectively with the phone volume the receptionists were handling. Since the reception desk seemed amply staffed, we were perplexed. But after observing the front desk for a few hours, there was no denying that the phones were very busy—and the overload was impacting more than just copay collection. Other tasks like checking patients in and updating the EHR so that clinicians would know patients were ready were also slipping through the cracks or not being done promptly.

As we observed and interviewed staff, we learned that the reception desk hadn't always been overburdened with calls. Previously, a phone tree had helped isolate prescription refill calls—which amounted to more than 80% of call volume—and connect them directly to the nurse who handled those requests. But the doctor had noticed that the front desk staff seemed to have a lot of down time, and thought this was an inefficiency that needed to be addressed. (The doctor's office was right next to the front desk, so he couldn't help but notice the idle time. The profitability of his busy practice didn't seem to be increasing at the same pace as his workload. If all staff weren't fully utilized all the time, wasn't that part of the problem?)

Eager to get more productivity from the receptionists, the doctor asked the manager to turn off the phone tree. Why should patients calling in reach an automated system when the receptionists had downtime? The doctor thought his solution would not only ensure he got maximum value from front desk staff, but also make patients happier. Who wouldn't prefer to reach a human instead of a machine?

After the change, the doctor felt much better when he looked out of his office at the front desk and saw staff constantly working. Patients, on the other hand, felt worse. With the phone tree, they had been able to quickly direct themselves to the prescription desk. Now they were often put on hold by the busy receptionists, and even when they weren't, they still had to explain why they were calling in order to be transferred to the prescription nurse.

Worst of all, now that the receptionists were constantly answering phones and transferring calls, there was no capacity for the much more profitable task of collecting patient payments—or for other important tasks the front desk had previously helped out with, such as one-off marketing projects, patient surveys, scanning, and mailings.

While it annoyed the psychiatrist to see the receptionists occasionally idle, the problem he solved wasn't really a problem. Simply making the receptionists *busier* would not make them more productive. More important, by making the refill process less efficient and depleting the resources available for more valuable tasks (like the crucial task of collecting patient payments) the psychiatrist had unwittingly made his practice less profitable. The practice was also less able to deal with unexpected surges in demand, since all the slack at the front desk had been absorbed.

Eyes on the prize: productivity

Distracted by the seemingly underutilized employees under his nose, the psychiatrist thought only of making them busier, without evaluating whether this would truly make them more *productive*. Workflow changes like these that are driven only by observations of "inefficiency" often create more problems than they solve. Before making a change to practice workflow, consider how it would contribute to your practice's success. What are the goals your practice wants to achieve—and will the workflow change you're contemplating help you achieve them?

Your practice goals are the objectives that serve and define your practice's mission—and your own goals as a practice manager or physician owner. You may phrase them differently—but a practice's most fundamental management goals typically include:

- A consistently profitable practice
- Better service and the ability to provide quality care for more patients
- Satisfied patients and referring physicians who bolster the practice's reputation and happily refer new patients

Improvements to specific processes in your practice—e.g., "making the triage process more efficient" or "streamlining the referral process" —

really only add value to the extent that achieving them helps you meet overall practice goals. Fiddling with processes in ways that don't contribute to the goals of the practice is at best a distraction that prevents you from doing more productive tasks (now, or down the road). At worst, it leads to greater inefficiency than before you made the change.

The Goal

A wonderful book that illustrates this principle in a clever way is *The Goal* by Eliyahu Goldratt. A physicist and somewhat-accidental management guru, Dr. Goldratt used the fictional journey of a plant manager named Alex to show how identifying the key constraints in a cycle is essential to making changes that can have a positive impact on productivity. The book reads like a thriller—will Alex figure out how to improve his plant's productivity in time to save his job and save the business?—and, besides introducing the key concept of the *theory of constraints,* it's a fun and easy read. (In case it's not obvious: I highly recommend *The Goal.*)

In *The Goal,* Alex finally visualizes the importance of identifying the primary constraint—also known as the bottleneck—after going on a scout camping trip with his son. As the troop made a long hike into the woods, Alex noticed that a frustrating pattern repeated itself: the faster boys and troop leaders would get so far ahead that they'd eventually have to wait for the rest to catch up. Ultimately, the troop could only hike as fast as the slowest camper, regardless of how far ahead the faster campers tried to pull the group.

The fundamental idea was that the weakest link determines the strength of the chain. But Alex noticed something else that was less intuitive. He realized that the faster campers instinctively tried harder and harder to get ahead, even though they couldn't help the troop as a whole move faster. The only way the faster campers could help the entire troop was to help the slowest boys speed up. The slowest camper in the troop had physical limitations that meant he would never be as fast as the tallest, fittest campers—but the faster campers could help him by carrying his backpack.

The key to improving the troop's overall speed was being willing to *slow down* the fastest members: Lightening the load of slower boys would make the average pace of the troop much faster, even though the fastest campers would be going much more slowly.[16]

This insight was powerful for Alex in light of the process problems at the factory. For years, managers on his team had focused on pushing each department in the system to its maximum productivity and efficiency. Everyone assumed that this would add up to the most efficient process for the entire plant. But continuously improving the performance of the fastest parts of the process (the "speediest hikers") didn't change the fact that the slowest process held up the entire system—it just pushed the teams further out of sync with each other. Improving each process separately actually added to the stress on the entire system—especially on its most constrained processes—and made overall production slower. As inventory piled up at earlier stages in the process, storage costs increased, too, even leading to write-offs of parts that would never be used.

CASE STUDY: The booming pediatric clinic

A few years ago, my colleagues and I worked with a walk-in pediatric clinic that lived through an experience similar to Alex's in *The Goal*. The

---

[16] Why is this simple idea sometimes counterintuitive? I think perhaps because we commonly think of averages pulled up by higher values; however, in a dependent process, the overall speed isn't an average, but a limit defined by the slowest link.

clinic was led by a charismatic, ingenious physician who had bucked conventional wisdom by serving a patient base that was nearly 90% Medicaid patients (in one of the country's most Medicaid-resistant cities, no less). And she was not just succeeding with her brave venture—her five-PA clinic was growing like a weed, and she loved the opportunity she had created for herself to make a real difference in patients' lives.

Of course, with growth often comes growing pains, and the pediatric clinic had its share. Managing patient flow became more challenging as the practice grew. The physician was concerned about the amount of time it took her young patients to work their way through their clinic visits, which were growing longer—too long for many of them to cooperatively sit still. Even though the parents would have preferred shorter visits, they rarely complained: They were mostly grateful for the opportunity to visit such a welcoming and accessible clinic. The patients, on the other hand, were a handful. When faced with waiting times of up to an hour to see their PA, the kids would get restless—frequently running around the clinic and finding their way into places they weren't supposed to be. This was becoming a huge problem for the practice, because patients were making a mess, even sometimes breaking things, and the physician was worried about the expense and liability.

As part of her strategy for managing her practice's growth, the doctor hired an experienced practice administrator, Andrea, to help establish new procedures to speed up the practice's workflow, along with implementing more robust infrastructure (e.g., billing and EHR). By the time we arrived, many steps had been taken to make the practice's operations more robust. Andrea had also begun to tackle the biggest challenge: total cycle times for patients that reached two or three hours in some cases, even when patients presented with relatively minor complaints.

Having had some experience with Lean thinking, and having implemented workflow improvements in previous practices, Andrea set out to find inefficiencies in the practice flow. She smartly sought input from the various teams that helped manage patients as they made their way through their clinic visits: greeting and check-in, triage, the medical assistants that helped the PAs, the referral manager, and, of course, the PAs themselves.

Everyone agreed that the triage process was remarkably slow—and that the problems seemed easy to fix. Taking vitals, documenting patient complaints, and determining if the patient was due for a complete physical were taking over 20 minutes, mainly because the two triage nurses needed to share equipment and didn't have their own laptops in their rooms. The triage nurses—actually MDs from outside the US who were working towards re-licensing—were highly motivated to streamline their process. They suggested portable, compact machines that could capture all vital signs, along with a laptop for each room.

With these improvements, the triage process went from a 20-25 minute process to a 5-10 minute process—seemingly a clear victory for efficiency and improved cycle time. But something unexpected—and undesirable—happened instead. Patient wait times actually became longer—especially in the exam rooms. The problem of impatient young patients actually got worse.

A look at patient flow before and after the change explains why.

As the next diagram shows, to start, triage was one of four main steps in the patient flow—at 20 minutes, the second longest. Once patients were seen by the triage nurses, they were usually roomed immediately, and waited in the exam room about 15 minutes to be seen.

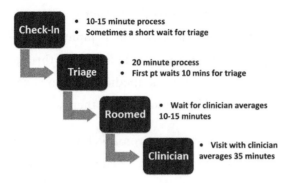

After the change in process, patients were also usually roomed quick-ly after triage. But, now all the time 'saved' was transferred to extra waiting time in the exam room, because the longest process—the bottleneck—was still the time spent with the PA.

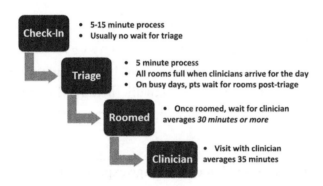

Instead of reducing the problem of patient wait times, the change made no difference in overall cycle time, and significantly worsened the most annoying part of the process: waiting in the exam room. (The roomed kids who were waiting more than 10 minutes were the most likely to get fidgety, poke their heads out into the hallway, and eventually slip out and nose around where they didn't belong.) In some cases, this even led to the actual encounter time taking longer as well, because the PAs and MAs had to look for restless patients who'd scampered out of their exam rooms and were being chased by their parents or hiding elsewhere in the clinic.

Of course, once we helped Andrea understand the new problem the change created, it could be quickly remedied. Speeding up the triage process without considering the impact further along in the cycle caused problems, but now that the practice knew where the real bottleneck was, they could take advantage of the nursing resources the change freed up to help the PAs complete visits more quickly.

They found lots of ways for the triage nurses to alleviate pressure on the bottleneck. For example, the nurses could follow a protocol to administer needed tests (strep tests, for example, were needed for as many as half the patients at some points in the winter) and vaccines, without waiting for the PA to find them and tell them to do so during the encounter. And the practice was able to cut down from two triage nurses to one during slower times, to avoid cycling patients into exam rooms too quickly.

One of the most direct ways to address the bottleneck would have been to add PAs or NPs—but, as is often the case with busy practices, this wasn't an easy option for the clinic due to space constraints. However, in addition to making the current group of PAs more efficient, Andrea also began exploring possibilities for additional weekend or evening hours that could expand clinician capacity somewhat.

Once it became clear that the *only* improvements that would speed up the patient process were ones that allowed clinicians to work more quickly, Andrea and the team had many ideas for how to make meaningful changes. Best of all, our work with Andrea to map out the practice's patient flow helped her reconsider how to measure performance and target changes more effectively in the future. As she continues her work to make encounters more efficient, at some point the clinicians may no longer be the constraint—and Andrea will now know how to find the new bottleneck to continue her improvements to patient flow.

Spotting bottlenecks: data gathering

Shouldn't the practice have known that—at 35 minutes on average—clinician time with the patient was the clear bottleneck in the process? While it might seem obvious as described here, in real life bottlenecks are not always so stark.

Picture yourself in an extremely busy walk-in clinic with many clinicians, each using three or four exam rooms to serve patients as they arrive (sometimes in waves) on a first-come, first served basis. Some patients will go through much more quickly than others, confounding your ability to estimate. It will be a lot easier to notice 'glaring inefficiencies'—like an easily streamlined triage step—than to get a holistic view of your entire workflow.

This is why there is no substitute for actually timing your processes—and gathering enough data to get a clear, numerical picture of your patient flow. (Call it evidence-based workflow analysis, if you will.)

Wait times are a critical clue to the bottleneck(s) in your system—as we can see with each patient's path through the pediatric clinic, diagrammed on the next page:

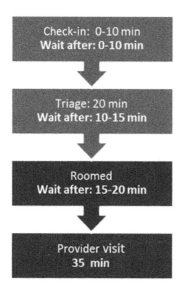

The longest stage—the visit with the clinician—is the bottleneck in the system; unless and until the clinicians can be made more efficient, patients won't go through the cycle more quickly, even if the other stages of the process are improved.

If your EHR adds time stamps as staff moves patients through the practice and allows you to report on the data, finding the slowest step of the process will be much easier. (Just make sure that the time stamps actually occur when processes end, to be sure you're able to calculate waiting times accurately. Sometimes, we see busy staff enter multiple all data at once—so it could look, for example, like the patient was checked in and roomed at the exact same time. Staff may not be aware of the value of this data, or how you'll use it; make sure they understand that accurate workflow data is a way to get payback from the extra effort of using the EHR.)

If you're not able to gather this data from your EHR—or, if you just want to get a clearer picture, up-close-and-personal, of your actual practice flow—manual time studies are another way to go.

"Time study" is a consulting term for following patients as they proceed through your practice and documenting the timing of each step of your flow. Collecting this data is a great task for consultants—we can observe the process all day long and be unobtrusive—but, you can do it yourself. Just be sure you have enough time (you need to have enough data to get a clear picture of your average process time and wait time at each stage). You also need to be aware of the Hawthorne Effect, which is the tendency for employees to move more quickly when observed by their managers. If you do the task yourself, spend enough time to 'fade into the woodwork' and get an accurate picture of how things normally work.

However you acquire the data, tracking your patients from the start to finish will allow you to create a spreadsheet something like this:

Pt.	Arrived	Checked-in	Triage /Vitals start	Triage /Vitals done	Roomed	Provider	Discharged	Check-out line	Exit
Jan S	9:05	9:15	9:25	9:30	9:30	9:46	10:00	10:01	10:14
Dot P	9:40	9:50	9:59	10:06	10:17	10:40	10:50	10:51	10:59
Anne C	10:02	10:08	10:18	10:24	10:32	10:52	11:07	11:09	11:25
[...]									

	Check-in Process Time	Wait for Triage	Triage Process	Wait for Room	Wait for Provider	Encounter	Room to Checkout	Check-out Process
Avg times	9 mins	10 mins	5 mins	6 mins	20 mins	14 mins	1 min	13 mins

In this fictional example, the average process time for the encounter—averaging 14 minutes—makes it the longest step in the system, and the bottleneck. You can also see that the wait time before that stage, at 20 minutes, is the longest wait—and therefore a flag to the bottleneck at the physician stage of the flow.

CASE STUDY: The ambitious RN OB/GYN administrator

When someone who's been a productivity superstar is promoted to manager, it can be very hard for her to accept anything less than perfect efficiency from her team. But, that tendency can make it easier get distracted by solving problems that don't actually improve overall process flow, save money, or otherwise enable the practice to meet its goals.

Pamela, a newly promoted, smart, and highly motivated practice administrator, fell into this trap. Her brief experience as a manager at a small practice hadn't fully prepared her for the challenges at her new practice, which had recently undertaken a huge building purchase and office build-out, causing serious worries about profitability. The situation would have been a tough test even for a more experienced manager. Pamela was courageous and energetic, though, and ready to act to improve the bottom line.

Rooting out inefficiencies, especially in staffing, was the first goal Pamela and the physician owners agreed on. Even before Pamela was hired as manager, the physicians had become concerned about staff inefficiency, especially among their several RNs. The physicians had heard that other local practices were using mostly medical assistants instead of RNs in order to save money—as a result, they believed they were wasting anywhere from $5 to $15 per hour on RN salaries for roles that could be performed by MAs. This situation irritated the physicians. They felt that they had unwittingly boxed themselves into a more expensive staff arrangement. This was one reason they urged Pamela to focus on overspending as she looked for ways to improve profitability.

Herself an RN, Pamela was instinctively sensitive to waste in the RNs' roles, and immediately noticed a particularly inefficient utilization of their time. For many years, the practice had offered newly pregnant patients a detailed consult with an RN after their initial OB visit with their physician. The new maternity patients were grateful for the opportunity to quiz the nurses about all the things they didn't get to ask (or just forgot) during their physician visit. But the nurses were spending an hour on each of these sessions—and Pamela knew from her own experience as an OB nurse that this was excessive. She shared the physicians' concern that the nurses were wasting time—and possibly even milking the system in a way that was justified only because "that's what we've always done."

Together with the physicians, Pamela came up with a solution. Instead of the one-hour RN consult after the initial physician visit, the physicians would add an extra 15 minutes to the new maternity patient visits. The physicians all felt that they could easily handle the patients' questions by adding 15 minutes more to the visit. And because the new OB visits were almost always part of a global billing package, they reasoned that there was no financial impact to the change, which would permit them to trim the nurses' hours. With about 100 new maternity consults each month, Pamela calculated that this change would save the practice about $2,500 per month on nursing wages. Unfortunately, Pamela and the physicians envisioned only those savings, not the costs of the change, both financially and in patient satisfaction and retention.

Physician time=money

Pamela thought that eliminating the nurses' inefficient OB consultations would immediately improve practice profitability. But even though the physicians believed they could do the consultations in 25% of the time it took the nurses, all of the physicians were completely booked. That meant the extended OB sessions would cut into the time available for other visits. Extending 100 monthly OB visits by 15 minutes would mean roughly 50 fewer preventive care visits (or 100 problem-oriented visits, or some combination of the two) at the practice each month.

By reducing physician appointments, the new plan would mean a net loss of revenue—a direct conflict with the goal of improving profitability. The 100 nursing hours cut could have saved the practice about $2,500 per month—except that the 25 physician hours lost in exchange had a potential value of more than $6,000. Because the OB consults were typically part of a global maternity billing package, there was no additional revenue generated by the extra physician time invested.

Even worse, it wasn't always possible to cut the nurses' schedules to reclaim the maternity consult hours, because the nurses still needed to be present in the office for their other duties. All told, the new approach would actually cost the practice at least $70,000 in profit per year—or about $14,000 in compensation per physician.

The change—perceived as an attack on the nurses—also crushed office morale. Patients were unhappy, too. New maternity patients who had heard from friends about the extra attention they'd get at Pamela's practice were disappointed to find the special consults were discontinued. And other patients were disheartened to find that wait times for a wellness visit or to resolve a problem were worse than ever. The practice lost money—and patients—at a time when it could least afford to.

Starting at square one

Pamela knew that her practice needed to be more profitable to support higher building expenses. Both Pamela and the doctors assumed that "cutting inefficiency" was the way to more profitability—her first misstep in defining the problem to solve. Profit is a function of both expenses *and* revenue. Practice managers and physicians frequently skip an analysis of the revenue side of the equation, but it often deserves more attention and can deliver a much bigger profit improvement. The right question usually is how can you get more patients flowing through your practice?

If Pamela had considered the complete process of cycling patients through the practice—from visit to revenue collection—she would have learned that patients were already waiting at least 90 days for wellness appointments, and problem-oriented visits were scarce as well. The wait time for appointments was the real bottleneck that Pamela should have analyzed before jumping on a perceived inefficiency.

What's more, had Pamela checked benchmarks for OB/GYN practices, she would have realized that her physicians were seeing many fewer patients on average than others in their specialty. Even though the physicians seemed busy—and overbooked—they were not managing to see as many patients as they could. This would have led her to look at the biggest opportunity to improve profitability: better scheduling.

In recent years more patients had come to rely on the practice for primary care—hence the demand (and opportunity) for more wellness visits. But no one had evaluated the established time slots to determine if the mix was appropriate. Additionally, patients were delaying pregnancy because of the slow local economy, so OB visits were down. Too many slots were reserved for maternity care—meaning that sometimes the "overbooked" physicians actually had openings on days they were in the office. Moreover, patients who would have been willing to see one of the practice's less-booked NPPs for their annual appointments were not consistently offered the option—instead they were booked for appointments months later with their assigned physician.

The practice also had a terrible no-show rate—nearly 20%. No one had examined their reminder process in years—and it was failing miserably. A few quick tweaks—collecting cell phone numbers and email addresses for electronic reminders, implementing automated reminder calls, experimenting with timing—had the potential to bring in several additional patients per day, at no additional cost. These types of easy fixes—focused at the point of congestion, appointment access—would bring in much more revenue than could ever be 'saved' by cutting nurses hours.

Not every problem needs a workflow solution

Pamela's goal was to make the practice more profitable, but she assumed that meant expense reduction. Her biggest mistake was not looking at the entire process flow to determine whether more patients could be seen. Had she started there, she would have quickly recognized the bottleneck in scheduling that was severely depressing the practice's revenue.

But Pamela made another mistake—a very common one. When she decided that the nurses were taking too much time with OB patients, she compounded her error by changing the workflow to address the issue. She believed the nurses were deliberately dilly-dallying. Yet the nurses had done the consults this way for years—and had no reason to believe the extra attention they were giving to the patients was a problem. (In fact, they assumed the opposite, since their patients raved about the extra care.)

Conflict avoidance, combined with the incorrect focus on 'waste' and expense cutting, led Pamela to make a decision that was very costly for her practice. Besides the immediate decrease in revenue, she missed out on the opportunity to learn why the nurses were giving hour-long consultations, to hear how well-received they'd been by patients, and to understand how committed the nurses actually were to the practice. The nurses also had many good ideas for how to improve the practice's relationships with patients—if only someone would ask. Pamela effectively cut off communication with her team, when, as a new manager, she really needed their support and input.

The second big lesson for Pamela: Don't make workflow changes to fix personnel problems. As she learned, workflow changes have profound domino effects. Her seemingly small change to the OB visits cost the practice *dozens* of visits and thousands of dollars. Never make a workflow change without analyzing the impact on your entire process flow.

Are clinicians always the bottleneck?

It's not always the case that the doctors are the bottleneck that keeps your practice from seeing more patients. But there is no situation in which making the doctors *less* efficient will make a practice more profitable.

In fact, it's fair to say that clinicians *should* be the bottleneck—and that you should always be looking for ways to make them more efficient, to make it easier for them to see more patients without compromising their care standards.

Physicians and NPPs are the main revenue generators in virtually every medical practice. Keeping them busy with *billable* work is critical to practice profitability. Adding non-billable tasks to their office workload—as Pamela did—is a surefire way to make your practice less profitable.

Sometimes, it can appear that physicians are maxed out—as they should be—but they actually are not. This was the case in Pamela's practice, which had scheduling problems that made it seem as though the physicians couldn't see more patients. One of the surest ways to verify whether clinicians are the bottleneck in your patient flow: Determine who is waiting.

When physicians and NPPs are truly the bottleneck—as in the pediatric clinic example—patients are almost always waiting for the physician or NPP to come to them, and rarely, if ever, the reverse. When physicians frequently wait for patients—whether because of no-shows, lack of demand, poor scheduling, or delays in moving patients through to exam rooms—they're less productive than they could be. For profitability, your goal should be to remove every obstacle to your physicians' productivity, making them the bottleneck in your workflow—and then continuously improve support systems to help them to stay as focused as possible on the work that only they can do.

CASE STUDY: Scheduling in a vacuum

Fred, the scheduling manager at a busy, 40-physician cardiology practice, and his practice administrator, Joanne, had a complicated and exasperating scheduling problem. The scheduling department was overwhelmed by a tidal wave of phone calls, primarily due to huge recall lists. One of their physicians had more than 300 patients per month on his recall list alone. Not surprisingly, some of the schedulers' inbound calls were complaints about access.

Despite the huge recall lists for many of the doctors, the schedulers also had to contend with frequent no-shows, which added to outbound calls for rescheduling. Oddly, even though so many patients were frustrated by scarce appointments with their physicians, other clinicians were underbooked, especially the newer physicians and PAs.

While Fred's team sometimes tried to improve access by scheduling more appointments with the underutilized clinicians, patients usually insisted on seeing the physician they'd seen before. New patients were also reluctant to see anyone except the doctor they were referred to—usually one of the physicians with a huge backlog. Consequently, some of the schedulers simply gave up on booking the newer physicians and PAs to save time on the phone; patients were worked in when possible, or either put on the recall list or booked weeks later than they should have been. Everyone at the practice was concerned that some referred patients who needed same-day appointments were not getting seen promptly enough.

Fred was desperate to reduce the stress on his schedulers, who were leaving the practice in droves. Every time a scheduler resigned, the problems faced by the remaining team members (and patients) became even worse. A downward spiral of diminishing access and patient dissatisfaction was well underway. The physician owners were pressing Joanne and Fred for solutions, too. Joanne and the physicians saw the scheduling issues as "Fred's problem," but also wanted to support him as he strived to solve it.

Overwhelmed by phone volume

Fred was certain that the phones had to be the focal point of any solution. The team was making outbound calls all day long to try to schedule the recalls; meanwhile, call-backs for scheduling and rescheduling booked appointments, calls for new appointments, and calls from frustrated patients on the recall list poured in every day. The team was always worried about missing an urgent message, and patient complaints caused great strain. Something had to be done to get the volume under control.

Fred thought about adding staff—Joanne and the doctors were very open to this—but, with turnover at an all-time high, it was difficult just to maintain the current staffing level, let alone recruit and train new people.

Given the constraints, Fred considered ways to change the process flow in the scheduling department to provide some relief. He came up with the idea of scheduling by mail instead of by phone, to reduce the outbound calling load. Scheduled appointments would be pre-set by the scheduling team, and then mailed out to patients. Patients who needed to change appointments could call to do so. Patients who couldn't be scheduled would receive a postcard asking them to call in—schedulers would try to work them in to cancellation slots or assign them to other clinicians.

Fred knew that this change wouldn't yield perfect scheduling. Some patients would inevitably call in to change their appointments. But Fred hoped that by reducing outbound calling, he'd give the schedulers a shot at handling the inbound calls and call-backs better.

A bad situation made worse

In the weeks after switching to mailing pre-set appointments, Fred was dismayed to admit his new approach had backfired. The scheduling situation became even worse—and problems that Fred didn't see as connected to his new way of scheduling ballooned.

One of the biggest problems was a dramatic increase in no-shows. Patients weren't accustomed to receiving appointments by mail. Many of them ignored the mailings, assuming they were marketing materials or bills. (Concerned about HIPAA, Fred chose to send letters instead of postcards, with no text on the envelopes stating an appointment was inside.) Fred had expected that his team would still need to make a few outbound calls for no-show patients—but now each scheduler had to make several more every day. No-shows alone drove the outbound calls almost back to where they had been before they began pre-mailing set appointments.

Undelivered mail also necessitated more outbound calling. Dozens of appointment letters were returned undeliverable—had the patients moved, or were they deceased? Previously, schedulers could verify patient address information when calling to schedule appointments. Many of the appointments mailed out were for one-year or six-month follow-up visits–a lot could change in a year. Undelivered appointment letters meant that the upfront work scheduling those appointments was wasted—and the patients weren't seen on time. It also meant another wave of unanticipated outbound calls was needed.

Inbound calling for rescheduling also increased dramatically. Like most cardiology practices, Fred's practice's patient base was primarily elderly people. Many had a hard time adapting to the new approach. Setting appointments by phone had been an important reassurance for them; some who more-or-less understood the new system called in to confirm anyway, just to be sure, adding to the phone volume.

The practice also had multiple locations, and the schedulers used them all to try to match as many patients as possible with open appointments with their physicians. But many patients had transportation issues that restricted them to one time or location. Calls from these patients flooded in as well.

Last but not least: the team's efforts to use the underutilized clinicians also caused a minor backlash. When patients were scheduled with a doctor they hadn't seen before, they called to reschedule with their prior physician in about 80% of the cases. And when they were scheduled with a PA instead of their physician, that number approached 100%—even when the visit was just a routine follow-up.

Limited view, limited effectiveness

Fred should have been able to anticipate some of these problems. He was so focused on the first-level problem of phone overload, though, that he neglected to think through what would happen once they started mailing pre-set appointments.

Everything in scheduling is interconnected. This helps make scheduling one of the toughest parts of your patient flow to successfully improve. Every change has the possibility of triggering a problem in another part of the system. Simple diagrams can help you think through what happens after each step. For example, Fred could have mapped out his process to recognize that mailing the cards would trigger not just patients showing up on time for their pre-booked appointments; it would also trigger calls to reschedule, returned mail, and no-shows. Knowing this, he could have had an idea whether the work on the back-end would exceed the time savings in outbound calling. He also could have considered a pilot program to test the effectiveness of the idea, to learn what problems might arise.

Mapping the process effects of his mailing idea would have helped Fred avoid the problems it caused. But while that might have helped him re-think his mailing idea, it couldn't have led him to a better solution to his practice's enormous scheduling issues. That's because Fred was empowered only to act within his own department, while many of the roots of the problem were beyond the schedulers' control. Fred was stuck with trying to solve a problem his department had little to do with causing.

Fred actually understood some of the issues that weren't under his control. For example, Fred's schedulers tried to book the new doctors and PAs to absorb the visit backlog, but gave up when patients resisted. Without urging and reassurance from their current physicians, patients are likely to fear seeing someone new, and especially seeing a PA instead of a doctor. Fred simply could not solve this problem without help and support from the physicians. Yet many of the most overloaded physicians were reluctant to refer their patients to others, even for low complexity visits.

Additionally, the practice had recently set up a new location, and Joanne had planned for all of the doctors to spend several weeks there each quarter. The idea was to reduce the overcrowding in the other clinics—in theory a plan that would help with the scheduling problems. But the new site was unfamiliar to many patients and inconvenient for others (it was more than 10 miles away from the practice's main office). When Fred's team scheduled patients at the new clinic, many called to switch to one at one of the other sites, and many others mistakenly showed up at the wrong location. The net effect was that the available visit slots for the busiest clinicians was substantially reduced—and, frustratingly, many of slots they had available for the new location went unused. Fred could see the way this problem was contributing to the recall problem for the busiest physicians, but had no way to address it on his own.

There were also substantial differences in physician behavior and preferences that impacted scheduling. For example, the practice didn't rely on a single protocol for follow-up visits—even for very common procedures and conditions. The schedulers therefore needed to know which doctors wanted to see patients at three months, which at six months, etc. Some of the doctors were also willing to work urgent cases in on the same day, while others were not—another point of scheduling customization that made scheduling for 40 clinicians more difficult.

Lastly, there were technology challenges. The practice's outdated robocalling reminder system was unreliable, and didn't allow for multiple phone numbers or texting. Worse than that, even though the system produced detailed reports about disconnected numbers and no-answer calls, the IT manager didn't share them with Fred.

Joanne and the physician owners had pledged to support Fred in his efforts to fix the scheduling problems. But what Fred really needed was their *involvement* in the solution. Patient flow problems invariably touch on multiple points in the process. It's critical for practice managers and physician leaders to get everyone working together to fix them—and to look at work flow holistically. Even though scheduling managers like Fred are often tasked with fixing workflow problems all by themselves, it's usually a losing battle when the causes extend beyond the scheduling department.

The big picture

One of the biggest pitfalls in improving workflow is looking at it as a collection of pieces—because it often seems natural to focus on just the part that seems 'broken.' This is especially true when practices grow large enough to have different departments and teams working on different parts of the workflow.

When you change workflow without doing an analysis of the entire flow from beginning to end, you're more likely to have unintended consequences. Even when the problem seems restricted to one area—as with Fred's scheduling stresses—the root causes may be elsewhere. And any attempt to solve the problem 'in a vacuum' at the trouble spot could simply transfer the difficulty to another point in the workflow, potentially making the situation even worse.

The need to look at workflow as an interdependent system means that leadership from the top is essential to solving workflow problems. Everyone in the practice has an interest in fixing these problems, even when only one area seems to be suffering. Unhappy patients and inefficient scheduling of clinicians hurt the entire practice. Employees who are 'in the weeds' often cannot see all the interconnected steps contributing to their problems. They also may lack the authority to make needed changes outside their areas of responsibility.

Regardless of practice size, the manager or administrator at the top of the staff organization chart is in the best position to gather all of the needed information. In smaller practices, the practice manager is positioned to know how each role in the workflow functions and interconnects. In larger organizations, the administrator can build a cross-department team to map out the entire system of processes and decisions, to home in on the bottlenecks that limit productivity and create hassles for patients and staff. By personally leading the effort and building the team, the administrator can be sure that all the necessary knowledge is pooled in the effort. The administrator can also protect against blaming and passing-the-buck, and urge everyone to work together to solve the problem.

Examining workflow from the top of the administrative side of the organization is essential to getting the complete picture—but physician involvement is critical, too. Patient flow is the intersection of the clinical and administrative side of the practice. Improving it often requires help and cooperation from the practice's clinicians, and that requires support and encouragement from the physicians at the top.

CASE STUDY: The business-savvy PCP

In my work as a medical practice management consultant, there's nothing I enjoy more than knowing that information I've shared has helped a practice become stronger and more profitable. But on the flip side, it's painful to learn of misunderstood management ideas doing harm to a practice. Unfortunately, this was the case with one of our most energetic and innovation-minded clients, who assumed that workflow advice that applied to other practices also applied to his primary care practice—with expensive consequences.

This compassionate doctor had a problem common to primary care physicians. He was overloaded with patients, and wanted to find a way to bring more patients in sooner.

This doctor was dedicated to improving patient access—and to improving his practice business in every way possible. He attended conferences. He read management books. He kept on top of practice management magazines and blogs. And he learned a lot.

Unfortunately, though, not every tidbit that gets published applies to every practice. Sometimes, your practice is already doing well at tasks that bedevil others. Measuring and evaluating before implementing solutions is essential.

Our client doctor had read about how patient flow can be restricted when there aren't enough exam rooms for all of the clinicians. This has been a frequent theme of practice management consultants over the past 15 years—and it's typically relevant to older practices stuck with outdated floor plans with large, separate physician offices and two or fewer exam rooms per doctor. In these situations, it's often possible to dramatically improve patient throughput by simply converting space that is used for private offices into exam space, perhaps even enabling the practice to add another physician or NPP.

But our eager client's practice didn't have such problems. He had three exam rooms, all well-designed, and they weren't impeding his ability to see patients. He didn't typically wait for patients to be roomed—they were almost always waiting for him.

Despite the fact that patients were ready for him before he was ready for them in almost every case, and despite the protestations of his office manager, the doctor was convinced that adding exam rooms would work the same miracles for him as it did for the doctors in dramatic case studies he'd read. And he didn't want to start small and risk missing out on any upside: instead, he reworked a huge part of his office space to double his exam rooms, from three to six.

Unfortunately, what happened next was predictable: longer patient wait times in the exam rooms. The doctor thought that if staff just queued up the patients in the exam rooms, he could pick up his own pace, and work through them all more quickly than when there were only three rooms. But he was already working at capacity, and adding the rooms did nothing to change that. Now patients were enduring longer waits where they hated them most. Not to mention the cost: the remodel had cost thousands of dollars and had disrupted the practice for weeks.

Ultimately, this story had a happy ending: The doctor eventually decided he should bring in another physician to use some of this new space. Luckily, he was flexible enough to expand his practice vision beyond working as a solo doctor. Still, a lot of unnecessary hassle, disruption and inconvenience to patients could have been avoided if he'd understood not all business advice applies to every practice—especially when it comes to the tricky business of changing your workflow.

The takeaways

One of my best bosses from my corporate career had a favorite phrase: "Never mistake activity for progress." He understood that being busy and being productive were two different things—and that being busy with unproductive tasks can deplete resources that could be better used on productive opportunities yet to come. This was the main take-away from the *Superstar Psychiatric Clinic*. The 'glaring inefficiency' right in front of you—the one that bugs you so much you feel you just *have* to fix it—well, it just might be red herring. Busy may not mean productive.

With the *Booming Pediatric Clinic*, we learned a fundamental lesson of workflow improvement: the importance of identifying the bottleneck to improve overall throughput. Changing the inefficient triage process before analyzing the entire process flow led to an unpleasant surprise. Since the triage process was not the bottleneck, making it faster didn't improve flow and actually made wait times longer. Eventually, the clinic was able to capitalize on the nursing resources freed up by streamlining triage—and put them to work helping to make the clinicians (the real bottleneck) more efficient. But the bumps in the road the change caused could have been avoided by mapping out the entire flow before acting.

A similar lesson was learned by Fred in *Scheduling in a Vacuum*. Mapping out the before and after flow of patients through your practice—or even just through your department—is the best way to avoid surprises. Even more important, though, is analyzing the *entire* patient flow before acting. In larger practices, it's common to isolate problems and make departmental leaders responsible for fixing them. But, the interdependencies between patient flow tasks make it essential to look at the process holistically before making changes. When individual managers are forced to solve workflow problems in a vacuum, they are often being set up to fail. Leadership from the top is critical. Practice managers are best positioned to coordinate a comprehensive analysis of the organization's entire workflow. But physician leaders must participate, too: Patient flow through the practice is the intersection of business operations and patient care.

The problems faced by Pamela, the *Ambitious OB/GYN Administrator*, illustrated another fundamental workflow takeaway: the importance of making revenue-generating professionals as efficient as possible. Make your clinicians less efficient, and your practice will be less efficient. Clinicians are the revenue engine of your practice. Even if they can do non-revenue tasks more quickly than a staff member, resist the temptation to capitalize on that 'efficiency.' Pamela's case also illustrated the importance of dealing with personnel issues directly. Addressing a personnel problem with a workflow change can easily lead to unintended consequences.

Our *Business Savvy PCP* taught us that business advice—whether about workflow, staffing, marketing, or virtually any other subject—is not one-size-fits-all. Before assuming what worked for one practice will automatically work for yours, measure and analyze. Sometimes you're doing better than you thought you were—even better than your peer group. And sometimes even when you have management challenges, changing your practice flow is not the answer to them.

PART FOUR

Modern Marketing: Basics of Online Reputation Management

Among the many dramatic ways the internet has changed our lives, one of the most significant is the ability to interact with services at any hour of the day or night. Whether you're buying a book from Amazon, ordering groceries, or booking a vacation, the internet lets you do it at 2:00AM, in your pajamas, if that's what's most convenient for you.

We're all getting pretty used to doing business like this—at our convenience, often without even speaking to another human. But, you may be thinking, isn't medicine a bit different? For sure, it's not typical for a patient to visit your practice "virtually," on-demand—at least not yet. A patient would be hard-pressed to find a physician's office open in the middle of the night. But that doesn't mean your prospective patient won't start looking tonight for a doctor to book an appointment with tomorrow. Will she find information about your practice when she does that midnight search? And if she does, what exactly will she find?

In our work at Capko & Morgan, we still meet physicians and practice managers who don't see the value of managing their practice's online image. Sometimes they're convinced that the web doesn't matter because patients still book by phone and find their practices by referral. But even when patients are referred to you by other physicians or trusted friends and family, they will still likely look for you online, if only to confirm you're contracted with their health plan. And once they do that, reviews, ratings and other content about your practice are just a click away. Even if you think you're invisible to patients seeking reviews because you've "opted out" of managing your online image, patients will find something about your practice online. If you're not managing that information, what they see may be working against you.

Health plan directories, ratings sites, and other databases now dominate search results. It's much more likely that patients will be directed to these resources than to your own website when researching—even when they search for you by name. It's crucial to know what is published in these resources. Data that patients see about your practice—even basics like your address or phone—might be incorrect. Errors like that can needlessly cost you new patients, and needlessly deprive those patients of the benefit of your services.

It's time to give up on opting out and take control. It's a lot easier than you might think. The first step is to learn about all the places your practice can be (and probably already is) listed on the internet, and to learn how to make sure the information on those sites is correct.

SEO is no longer enough

It wasn't too long ago that your practice's website had a pretty good chance of landing on the first page of search results, provided you paid good attention to search engine optimization (SEO). But review sites and directories—including the search engines' own business listings—have proliferated, and now tend to dominate page one of search results.

The example below—first page results of a Google search for an OB/GYN in San Marcos, CA—is typical for a local search for a physician. Practices' own sites rarely top search results anymore. Instead, the most prominent results are usually reviews sites and directories: Healthgrades, Vitals, Yelp, and, most notably, Google's own business listings.

Google's own listings take up nearly half of the first page of these results. If you were to search on Bing and Yahoo!, the next biggest search sites, you'd see the same sort of thing on page one: their own directory listings keyed to a map, alongside other publishers' physician directories.

The bottom line: if you want to get found by prospective patients who are using a search engine to research physicians, an accurate, up-to-date presence in these directories is essential.

This is not to say that maintaining your own site's SEO is no longer helpful. It still can be—for instance, because some patients may review the second, third, and fourth pages of search results. But it's not enough to ensure you'll be found when patients search in the most common ways for your specialty (or even your practice name). Maintaining your listings on directories that usually appear first in search results will help ensure that prospective patients will find you.

Directory reliability varies significantly

Publishers like Healthgrades, Vitals, and others offer huge amounts of content about physicians. This may explain why they've reached the top of search results so fast. But to efficiently create listings (also called profiles) of nearly every doctor in the US, they've relied on public sources like medical license databases. These sources often include outdated information. I've personally seen profiles with contact information and other details that haven't been true since the physician left residency or fellowship.

From the directory publishers' perspective, a few incorrect listings among thousands might not seem like such a big deal. They're aiming to provide a resource rich in options for patients—so what's the harm if a few details are out of date? Plus, they no doubt assume that doctors will eventually notice incorrect information. So instead of manually researching and correcting each listing themselves, they made it easy for physicians and administrators to find and edit their own profiles, through a process called "claiming." The claiming process empowers you to take control of listing information, but it shifts responsibility to you as well.

There is a bit of good news that comes along with this added responsibility, though. As you take control of your directory listing data, you usually get the opportunity to enhance your profiles as well. Many of these enhancements are free and can help you stand out versus your competition.

Online payer directories: essential and expanding

While independent directories like Healthgrades and Google or Bing's own directory listings top the search results, for many patients, payer directories are the most important step in an online physician search. A patient with coverage typically wants to use it. Before they call you, they'll want to be sure they can.

If you're not listed in the directory of a plan you participate in, or your listing incorrectly states that you're not accepting new patients, that directory is effectively turning prospective patients away from your practice. Directory errors silently but significantly undermine practice growth, because physicians and practice managers assume payers list them correctly, even though errors are common.

Out-of-date, inaccurate payer directories also harm patients who unintentionally see out-of-network providers—a common problem. In 2012, the attorney general in New York even launched an investigation into the issue.[17] Ultimately, numerous health plans in the state agreed to pay fines—and to implement systems to keep their directories updated. The case illuminated the poor reliability of payer directory information—and how difficult it appears to be for payers to keep directory information current. Yet despite the national attention it received, the ruling still hasn't done much to improve directory accuracy.

---

[17]See http://www.ag.ny.gov/press-release/ag-schneiderman-announces-settlements-requiring-health-insurers-publish-accurate

Nearly three years later, in late 2014, the California Department of Managed Care also found that errors were common in payer directories[18]. It found more than 18% of physicians' addresses listed incorrectly in one large payer's directory, and as many as 13% of physicians incorrectly listed as "in-network" in another.

Now California is taking legal action. California SB 137 sets requirements for directory accuracy by mid-2017. The bill aims to protect patients by holding payers liable for out-of-network costs due to listing errors. But the bill also permits payers to penalize physicians who don't promptly catch and report directory errors. Some payers are also including language in their "about" or "site policies" pages that explicitly shifts responsibility for listing accuracy onto physicians and other practitioners.

Here are just *some* of the damaging errors and omissions that are all-too-common in payer directories:

- Omitted from directory
- Missing subspecialty
- Incorrect address
- Outdated phone
- Missing secondary offices/locations
- Listed incorrectly as "not accepting new patients" (or vice versa)
- Improperly included in a dropped plan

Online payer directories once were typically hidden behind logins, so that only current plan members could access them. But with more patients shopping for plans online (especially since the individual mandate of the Affordable Care Act (ACA)), payers have begun opening up their directories online. Even Medicare has gotten into the act with its Physician Compare

---

[18]Among other sources, see Modern Healthcare's coverage at:
http://www.modernhealthcare.com/article/20141119/NEWS/311199972

website. As they receive more patient traffic, payer directories have more influence on patients' physician choices.

Payer directories have also started mimicking features of the physician reviews and ratings sites. Some plans encourage members to rate their physicians and search on others' ratings, as seen here on the Blue Cross/Blue Shield national directory:

United Healthcare (UHC) has also opted to include star ratings in its directory, and has partnered with Healthgrades to use theirs (another reason to make sure your listings at both sites are accurate). But an even more notable UHC feature is that they've begun encouraging patients to price compare. UHC's directory displays an "average" price range for a typical service in a geographic area, then states in each listing whether the physician meets or is above or below the range.

As patients become more cost-sensitive (thanks to increasing deductibles and other cost-sharing), and health plans encourage them to price-compare, this type of information will likely become more common in health plan directories. But if a plan incorrectly lists you as "above average cost," the plan's directory could discourage patients from contacting you. This is all the more reason to regularly inspect your listings in all your contracted plans' directories for accuracy and completeness.

Features of payer directories are evolving rapidly. Staying on top of how you're presented is imperative to ensure patients find you and receive correct information about you and your practice. As plan directories track and present more data, there are more opportunities for mistakes.

Hospitals have also been jumping in with their own online directories. Private practice physicians may be more likely to be omitted or listed incorrectly. Remember that patients may consult these directories when planning for needs like surgery or delivering a baby. Make sure you're properly listed in the directories of all hospitals you work at, so patients don't mistakenly assume you're not an option at their preferred one.

Wrangling your payer directory listings

Keeping payer directory listings updated requires effort, but it can mean immediate results in terms of new patients, especially if a key employer adds a plan in your area. As payer directories have become more open to the public in recent years, they've also become easier for you and your staff to surf and scan for errors.

That's the good news. On the bad side, unlike the standalone reviews and ratings sites, payer directories haven't evolved towards a similar process for correcting and enhancing your listings[19].

––––––––––––––––––––––––

[19]Part of California's SB 137 legislation addresses this issue. The Department of Managed Care and the Department of Insurance are required to develop uniform standards, working with payers. More states could follow suit, as they look for ways to deal with patient complaints about directories.

Every payer directory has its own scheme for fixing problems, and it can sometimes require a little detective work to figure out how to do it. But most of the time the answer will be one of the following:

- A link and form on the site that allows any visitor to submit errors;
- Access to your listing data through a separate physician portal;
- A link from within the directory listing itself to submit a correction;
- A general contact form to submit any type of problem with the website;
- If none of the above are options, you should be able to work through your account rep.

Maintaining directories is an excellent task to divide up among staff members, who can each work on their own directory(s) during down time. A good starting point is to engage your billing team to be sure you're registered with all of your payers' portals, since in many cases your directory listings will be maintained through your portal account. (Making sure you have portal accounts with all your payers is useful for other reasons, too—including keeping tabs on contract amendments and expirations.)

When planning your process for reviewing and updating payer directories, don't overlook Medicare and its Physician Compare site. To maintain these listings, you'll start with the NPPES/PECOS portal. The good news here is that you may already have a login that you set up when applying for your NPI number. But because the typical use of this portal is for managing Medicare credentialing, the data that appears for your practice may not reflect what patients need to know. For example, if you are part of a large group with a central office, the central office's address might display as your location—even if your clinic's not located there. If you have multiple practice locations, it's also possible that they will not all be displayed properly.

Fixing these types of problems on Physician Compare can take patience and persistence. Secondary addresses can be added through the PECOS system, but can take up to three months to display on Physician Compare. In some cases, you will need to email the service for assistance. But don't give up, and don't let up: Physician Compare was mandated by the ACA, and new information is being added at a fast clip. (The site already includes Meaningful Use, eRx, and PQRS participation information, and will report on their new implementations under MACRA.) The site is likely to become more important to consumers as it expands. And as it adds data from various sources, errors may be more likely. Keep an eye on it to be sure you're presented properly to patients insured by this key payer.

Another payer directory that requires special attention is the Blue Cross/Blue Shield national directory. This site often comes up at the top of results for searches like "blue cross physicians," regardless of the searcher's location. But the national site may not be updated when you change information with your local BC/BS affiliate. Even if you're certain your listings with the regional BC/BS affiliate(s) you contract with are correct, it's a good idea to monitor the national directory to be sure it's right too.

Partly in response to the directory legislation in California, a website called BetterDoctor.com has developed a software solution that allows practices to more easily update their listing information across multiple payer directories. Be sure to check out this site to learn how/whether it applies to your local market. As more plans connect through the BetterDoctor system, practices in other parts of the country should benefit from a more convenient way to update directory data.

Divide and conquer

Directory hygiene is a task that can easily be divided and shared by the entire front office team. With payer directories in particular, your billers and schedulers may have an edge in navigating the process, so involve them from the start. Set a time-frame for initial review and correction of all your plans, and then a regular schedule for checking and updating quarterly or twice per year. Make sure your team prioritizes the payers that you value most to be sure your listings are helping you attract more patients from those plans.

Include hospital directories in your planning

The task of finding, verifying, and correcting hospital listings fits well with managing payer directories. If an employee (such as a surgery scheduler or on-call scheduler) already has a relationship with your hospital, monitoring that hospital's directory data would be a natural extension of that employee's role.

Hospitals in some markets are increasingly ambitious with their directory efforts as they battle for search engine attention. Some are even adding reviews and ratings to provide a counterpoint to sites like Healthgrades and Vitals. But acquiring and maintaining accurate directory information is a challenge for any organization that's not in the directory business. If you find errors and are unsure how to correct them, the hospital's marketing or physician relations department is a good place to start.

Put yourself on the (Google or Bing) map

Google's very visible directory program, Google My Business, is the most important public directory to update and manage. Google's own directory listings routinely show up at the top of the results for medical practice searches. If a prospective patient starts with a Google search on your specialty and location, they're likely to be presented an array of Google business listings. Naturally, you'd like yours to be one of them—especially since Google is estimated to account for 60-80% of all U.S. web searches.

The next screenshot shows a typical local web search, this one for pediatricians in San Rafael, California. Notice that Google's map and its own listings, keyed to the map, are the first thing displayed after the paid advertisement.

Notice also how the map allows a searcher to immediately see if there is an option that is especially convenient to her. This gives the physicians shown on the map a big advantage. Besides being displayed high on the first page, the listings format also stands out.

Each of the listings in this group includes contact information, so the patient needn't click through to find the phone number and address. (And if the patient simply calls one of the numbers listed and books an appointment, all the other practices hoping to attract her have just lost their chance.) If the searcher does click through, she may find Google reviews, a Google+ page, or both. Google's listings draw upon what the practice publishes in their listing as well as other online information that Google has identified as connected to the physician.

It has always been easy to take advantage of Google's listing opportunities, and it seems to get incrementally easier and more intuitive with each new version[20]. It requires a little bit of effort, but offers a lot of upside. To get started with claiming and managing your Google listing, head to www.google.com/business. You can use the phone number provided to get help walking through the process, if you prefer, but the self-service option you'll launch by clicking "Start Now" is very easy.

---

[20]Google's directory program is constantly evolving, and the name has changed frequently. Since I began writing about online reputation management just a couple of years ago, the product has had two other names, Google Places and Google+ Local. By the time you read this, who knows, they might have changed the name again! But don't stress if they have: Google's process for redirecting users to new systems is typically very user-friendly.

You'll need a Google account to proceed. If you have an account already, but it's for personal use, select the option to create one using a practice email. (This is not just a good idea for your own privacy. In the unlikely event someone improperly attempts to claim your listing in the future, an address attached to your practice domain will carry more authority with Google in a dispute.)

Use a generic or multi-user email such as 'info@mypractice.com' if you have one (or can create one). With a generic business email, you'll be able to assign staff members or a third-party service to maintain the listing(s) for you but still be able to easily control access to the account.

Once you've chosen or set up a Google account, you'll be prompted to find your business in the directory. If Google already has a listing for your practice, you'll be able to track it down and claim it. If no one at your practice has taken steps to set up your listing, you may need to set up a new one, but more likely you'll find Google has already pieced one together for you using information from other directories. Pay special attention to this step if you or your practice could be listed at a previous address, possibly set up by someone else. Claiming that outdated listing will allow you to edit it and redirect searchers to your current address.

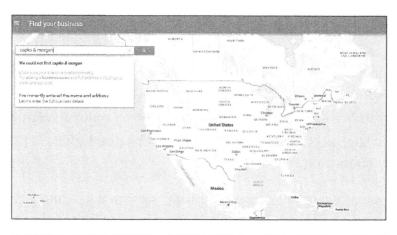

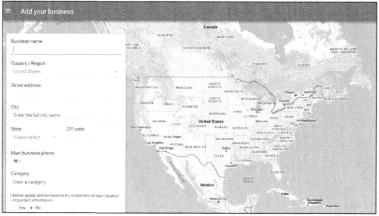

Finally, once you've entered your practice address and phone information, you'll be presented with a link to create your Google+ page, and asked to verify. You'll need to click a link that instructs Google to mail a card (with a verification code) to the address you've provided for the practice. Be sure to alert whoever checks the mail at your practice to watch for the card. (The cards can easily be mistaken for junk mail and discarded.) While waiting for the verification card, don't make any changes to the listing, since that might require restarting the verification process. If you're attempting to change a listing that includes an outdated address, you may need a helper to intercept the card for you at that prior address.

Once you've received the card (in 1-2 weeks), log back in to your Google account and enter the verification code to confirm your identity and claim the business listing. And that's it for claiming: you're done. You now control your listing and can update it as needed if you move, or add a phone number or website. You'll also be able to continue personalizing your Google+ page as you like. You can add photos, tagline, video, email contact information, etc.

Google's verification process usually goes without a hitch. The most common problem is the card not arriving or being missed, and that's easily rectified: just log in and request another. But if you're having trouble you can't resolve, Google's support forums often have the answer. And if the forums can't help—for example, if you've moved and can't receive the verification card at the published address—you can reach Google support from the support.google.com/business page, and generally get an answer quite promptly. (There's usually an option to get help via phone, rather than email, at a time that works for you. This can be much quicker than emailing back and forth for persistent problems.)

Continue the process with Bing

Once you've finished claiming and enhancing your Google listing and Google+ page, you'll have increased your chances of being easily found by the 70% or so of web users who start their web searches at Google. Repeating the process for Bing will help you reach most of the other prospective patients who start looking for a doctor via a search engine.

Bing's process is very similar to Google's. The easiest way to start is to search "bing places for business" or visit www.bingplaces.com. From there you'll walk through three steps to claim or add, enhance, and verify your Bing business listing.

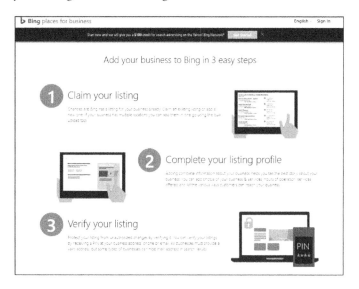

Don't forget to double-check after submitting

After your listing is submitted and verified, it's always a good idea to double-check that it posts correctly. Without knowing exactly how Google and Bing accumulate their data and attach it to business listings, it's impossible to prevent every error. Claiming or establishing your own listing and regularly updating it is your best defense. But errors can still happen. Checking that your listing posts properly after you set it up, then re-checking it periodically, is the best way to be sure your prospective patients aren't being directed to a competitor instead of your practice.

Physician reviews and ratings sites

Physician ratings directories—sites like Healthgrades and Vitals—are what many people think of first when thinking about online reputation management. These are the sites that gave the idea of patient ratings so much momentum. They have helped transform the way patients research physicians—but they've also rankled many physicians and managers, who are unsure that the idea of patient ratings is even appropriate.

If you've held back from managing your reputation on these sites, know that sitting on the sidelines limits only your influence, not theirs. These directories are populated with information from public databases. They don't need your cooperation to publish your listing, but, without it, they could publish incorrect details that can harm your practice business. If you instead engage with these sites, you'll be able to correct any errors. You'll also usually have an opportunity to polish your image by adding photos and other details.

The first step is claiming your listings by identifying yourself and taking control of your or your practice's listing information.

Most of the physician reviews and ratings sites make it pretty simple to claim your profile. Claiming typically involves providing a bit of unique identifying information to validate your authority to modify the listing. Usually, a few steps are required to confirm both the confidential data and your contact information, so that the site can be reasonably sure listings aren't tampered with or removed by third parties.

For example, the site may have accumulated information from various public sources about physicians' education (both undergrad and medical), licensing and provider ID numbers (state and national), specialty and current or previous contact information. They use your knowledge of this data to confirm you're the listed physician (or designee). If you're an administrator claiming listings for one or more physicians, it can be useful to have the following identifying information available before you start:

- Personal information: full name, date of birth
- Identifying numbers: NPI, DEA, state license
- Graduation dates and schools
- Addresses of current and past practice locations
- Specialty society or association memberships (and emails that might have been used to register)

I usually recommend most practices start their claiming efforts with the largest and most commonly used sites. Keep in mind, though, that there may be other, smaller sites that are focused on your specialty or local area; these may be even important to your prospective patients. Periodically searching like a patient would, and even asking patients how they searched for you online, is an easy way to keep on top of local changes. As more targeted sites emerge that could reflect on your practice, be sure to start monitoring and updating those listings as well.

Healthgrades

Healthgrades (www.healthgrades.com) is a prominent physician rating site in most markets. The site frequently shows at the top of searches, sometimes even above Google and Bing's own directory listings. Plus, it uses advertising and social media to increase awareness and continue to grow its large user base. To be sure you can tap into this large audience in a positive way, the first step is to verify that your information on the site is correct and reflects as positively as possible on your practice.

Start by clicking on the "physicians" link at the top right of the Healthgrades home page. (This is the place to start whether you're a physician, NP, PA, other clinician, or an administrator maintaining information for your entire practice.)

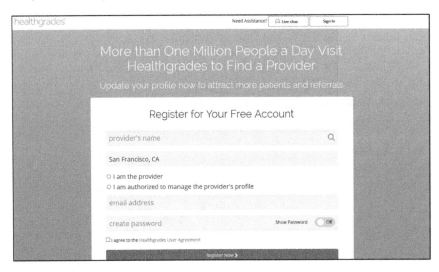

Once you click on the link you'll be asked to register and identify yourself as either a listed physician or an administrator authorized to maintain the physician profile.

If your physicians are part of a group practice that is already known to Healthgrades, good news: Healthgrades will automatically allow you to access all listings for the group. If your practice is not recognized as a group to Healthgrades, contact support and ask them to set up the group connections on the site, so that you can claim and edit the entire group.

Once you've registered and can edit your profile(s), you'll find Healthgrades has many detailed data sections to update. You'll be prompted to include not just general information about the physician, but also conditions treated, procedures performed, and insurance plans accepted.

These can be quite time-consuming to complete, so start with the most important things: Ensure all specialty and contact information is correct, then add a photo and, if available, a video. Work on the details of conditions, procedures and health plans bit-by-bit, as you have time (always prioritizing the most valuable of each category).

Why a photo first? Check out this sample page—a basic search on pediatricians in Palo Alto, CA. Notice how, even in black and white, one listing stands apart from the rest? Launch a search on almost any specialty in any community, and you'll see the same sort of thing: many listings with placeholder silhouettes instead of photos, and occasionally one or two listings will show up (more noticeably) with a photo.

Adding a photo to any online listing will improve your visibility. Just make sure it's a reasonably recent photo. If your photo looks too dated, it may stand out for the wrong reasons.

Vitals

Vitals (www.vitals.com) uses a claiming process that's similar to Healthgrades. But to get started on Vitals, you first need to find your listing and look for "claim profile" on the lower right side. Click on the link to register and create a password. Once registered, you'll be able to claim your profile by providing verifying information.

Like Healthgrades, Vitals allows patients to search on conditions as well as clinician name and specialty. Entering condition information can help your listing show up more frequently. This can be a significant opportunity to stand out versus other practices. Even competitors who've claimed their profiles may not have taken the more time-consuming step of entering conditions—especially if they don't realize how this data affects search results on the site.

For example, I recently did a Vitals search for "hypothyroidism" in Thousand Oaks, CA, and exactly *one* endocrinologist was returned. Yet a general search on "endocrinologists" returned 16 results in Thousand Oaks proper—and about 400 in the communities nearby.

This is by no means an isolated example. Many common conditions have few or no physicians attached to them on these directory sites, simply because no one has taken the time to enter the condition data. If you're just getting started updating your profiles on Vitals and Healthgrades, make time to chip away at the task of updating condition lists. Even a few minutes a week will get the job done eventually.

Get your Healthgrades and Vitals listings under your control, and you'll have made great strides towards increasing the accessibility and visibility of your practice. You'll be ready to track and respond to the ratings and reviews on these sites as well.

Once you've edited the top priority sites, give some attention to the 'second tier' of physician ratings sites. Your second tier may be different from practices in other markets, as local and regional sites may emerge that are important to patients in your area. Do a few searches based on how patients for services you provide, and see what sites appear in the top results.

Three prominent directories that often rank well for many areas and specialties are MD.com, UcompareHealthCare, and RateMDs.

MD.com (www.md.com) deserves a bit of extra attention because it has some unusually helpful features. MD.com not only allows physicians to include a link to their own site—an increasingly rare option—it also allows you to link to your social media presences. This is a great way to add personality to your profile on MD.com, help your own site's SEO, and attract new social media followers. Your page on MD.com is like a free, stripped-down, extra website for your practice. MD.com offers lots of ways for you to enhance your space, too. The site has recently added a telemedicine platform, online scheduling, and other premium services (for a fee) that may be worth checking out.

The claiming process is very straightforward—start at doctors.md.com or click on the 'Are you a doctor?' link on the home page. You'll need to have your NPI number and your cell phone (for text verification) to complete the claim.

UCompareHealthCare (www.ucomparehealthcare.com) also has a straightforward claiming process. Find your listing and click through to you profile, then click the "are you doctor x?" link near the bottom right; the link takes you to a page where you can select "edit basic profile" and make sure your basic data is correct (at no charge). (If you're not listed at all, UCompareHealthCare asks you send email marked "inclusion request" to info@ucomparehealthcare.com, with physician CV attached.)

RateMDs (www.ratemds.com) is a popular site that relies on users to create its listings. Unless a patient has submitted your practice with a review, you're probably not listed. But the site has recently added a claiming and submission process for physicians and managers. If you're not listed, adding your practice can be useful because of the site's visibility in search results. (And if you are listed, check the details carefully. Your listing was likely based on data submitted by a patient, which may not be correct.)

Specialty and local directories

Registering and claiming your listings on the physician directories profiled here is likely to give most practices a good shot at presenting correct information to patients searching for a new doctor. But I can't emphasize enough how important it is to do your own searches to find other sites I haven't covered that might be important in your local area or for your specialty. (Two specialty-focused examples: RealSelf.com for plastic surgery and cosmetic medicine, and ObesityHelp.com for bariatric surgery.) Periodically checking Google and Bing—searching like a patient—will help you stay on top of shifts in SEO, plus learn about new ratings sites. Ask staff to ask patients how they find you, and be sure to check your listing when you hear of a new online resource.

In some markets, for some searches, general business directory and rating sites like Yelp and Angie's List rank as well or even better than physician directories. These two sites may be very important to your patients—and thus very important for you to track. In fact, research by Software Advice, a software research and consulting firm, found that while Healthgrades was more used than the other physician ratings sites it surveyed, Yelp was more trusted[21]. If Yelp is popular in your area for other services, you may find it's very important for physicians as well.

To get started on Yelp (www.yelp.com), the first step is to register and claim your listing if it already exists on the site, or else create one. Start at biz.yelp.com, where you'll register and find your listing and claim it or start creating a new one.

Most of the time, the Yelp claiming process is straightforward, but there is one hitch that challenges practices: Yelp uses an automated phone calling system to validate your listing. Once you have entered your or corrected your contact information, Yelp will attempt to call your listed number to provide a PIN code to be used to complete the claim. This can be unworkable if your office uses a phone tree.

[21]See http://www.softwareadvice.com/medical/industryview/how-patients-use-online-reviews/

If your system uses extensions, you can enter one to be called directly with the PIN. Alternatively, you may be able to work around the problem by making your claim during off hours, if your phones aren't sent to an automated answering system or external service. If the available options don't work for you, contact Yelp support for help.

Angie's List (www.angieslist.com) reviews are only available to members, but that doesn't mean you can't claim your listing, complete and fix your profile, and monitor and respond to reviews. Start at their business center (www.angieslistbusinesscenter.com) and click 'claim your profile.' The process is typically straightforward, but if you have problems, you can get assistance both online (through FAQs in the support center), via email (using their contact form) and by phone.

New sites, new technologies: new opportunities

One of the challenges in managing your practice's online reputation is that the market for web services connecting patients with doctors is still pretty new. Innovation is still buzzing, and new sites and tools are still emerging frequently. The downside of all of this innovation is that it can feel hard to keep up. But the plus side is that as the category evolves, online resources tend to improve for both doctors and patients. New software and services, even new categories of services, have emerged that can make managing online data much easier for practices.

Here are a few of the technology innovations that I recommend you keep an eye on:

Reputation management software

One of the most exciting categories of front office technology to emerge in the past few years is reputation management software. These tools use APIs (application programming interfaces) to connect to directory sites, allowing practices to claim and manage multiple directory listings from a single dashboard. Many also offer online scheduling and integration with practice management systems. Systems that include online scheduling make it easy to 'close the loop' with patients after their visits—a boon for increasing the number of reviews of your practice.

There are a number of options currently in this category, including DoctorBase (part of Kareo), PatientPop, and Simple Interact. But this new, dynamic market is likely to see further innovation and change in the next few years. Besides checking out these options, ask your practice management system if they can recommend products that integrate with theirs.

Booking engine: ZocDoc

ZocDoc (www.zocdoc.com) is a booking engine that allows patients to schedule appointments directly with practices online—without a phone call. Because it caters to more urgent needs or patients searching for a new physician, it tends to be most useful for primary care (including pediatrics and OB/GYN). But the service does allow patients to search based on their insurance, which is making it more useful to other specialties.

Convenient booking on short notice is valued by patients, and practices benefit because gaps in their schedules are filled. But beyond these core benefits, ZocDoc is a powerful reviews engine that can give a serious boost to your practice's online reputation.

ZocDoc systematically contacts patients after they book a visit with a doctor and asks them for a rating and review. This process has enabled ZocDoc to build up a significant store of reviews and to compete with the reviews and ratings sites. From a practice's perspective, the reviews on ZocDoc have big advantage because they are verified. ZocDoc only gathers reviews from actual patients who booked with the practice and received service. This, in turn, allows practices who have received new patient leads from its service to see feedback from specific patients who are definitely theirs—patients they may even remember from a recent visit.

Perhaps partly because of its large base of reviews, ZocDoc also frequently appears near the top of search results. This helps the doctors who participate get found and booked via the service and helps ensure a practice's positive reviews get noticed.

If your practice (or one of your doctors) is not fully booked, ZocDoc may be a worthwhile investment. The ability to build up positive reviews (by ensuring your new patients have a positive experience) is a secondary factor that might help make the service a cost-effective form of marketing.

Pricing sites, estimators, and other services

Another area exploding with innovation is sites and apps that help patients choose practices based on pricing information, pay online, or estimate their financial responsibility. All of these services can negatively impact your practice's reputation if your information is inaccurate, unfavorable, or excluded.

A flurry of new startups (one example is Castlight) aims to help employers and patients choose doctors based on cost. But while they aim to guide smarter purchase decisions, these sites don't necessarily have access to accurate information about your pricing. In some cases, the sites may have drawn data from public fee schedules (i.e., charge masters) that don't apply to cash or insured patients—meaning patients may make decisions about your practice based on prices that are incorrect. Some payers are also joining this category, and posting fee schedules online for their members.

Working with these sites to verify your pricing information can expand your reach to patients while ensuring you're not misrepresented. Plus, you'll want to check for all the potential errors that can go wrong with any sort of directory—address problems, missing credentials, etc.—since they can occur on pricing sites, too. Some of these sites actually offer the opportunity for patients to pre-pay—another benefit to your practice. It's worth the effort of someone on your team to stay on top of new shopping services being launched for patients, to be sure you're represented well and not missing out on valuable exposure.

Avoiding and troubleshooting listing data problems

Moving? Claim any existing listings before you change addresses

Directory listings that point to outdated practice information will almost certainly cost you patients. That's not usually something a new practice or location can afford. If you're moving or starting a new practice, you'll likely be juggling all kinds of start-up challenges for many months. If you move before claiming existing listings, the process of identifying yourself as the rightful owner will likely be more difficult (especially for search engine listings that are verified by postal mail).

This is one more hassle you definitely won't need while starting up, and you'll absolutely want to be sure patients can find you at a new location. So be sure to claim your listings *before you move,* so that you'll control them and be able to change your address your move is complete.

Use forums and blogs for quick answers to questions and problems—be persistent

If you're experiencing a problem, search on a brief description of it on Google or Bing. Usually you won't be the only person experiencing the issue and an answer will be posted on a forum or blog. Directories also almost always have a help page or FAQ with information about common issues—and, failing that, they usually have contact information available. It may take more than one attempt to get an answer via an email or phone call, but someone will almost always eventually respond.

Be persistent if necessary. Unresolved issues can be as problematic for patients as for your practice—sometimes even more so. Thanks in part to healthcare legislation, more patients are dealing with unfamiliar coverage and increasing financial responsibility. When payer directory information is incorrect, it's easy for a patient to make a costly mistake and end up paying out-of-network costs. (Not to mention the revenue hit your practice might take.) Resolving problems can be frustrating, but it's worthwhile—even essential—to be persistent.

Enlist help and escalate unresolved problems

If patients repeatedly complain that your listing is incorrect in a directory, and you can't claim it and update it yourself, encourage them to report the error to the publisher. Most directories (both payer directories and ratings sites) have a "report a problem" link for this purpose, but even those that don't usually have a contact form. Problems that are reported via multiple sources may get more attention. Enlist friends to send a quick message if you're really having trouble getting help fixing an error.

Don't try to fudge

Be truthful in updating practice names, specialties, locations. Google, in particular, is aware of the temptation to spam by creating multiple listings, changing practice names, adding non-existent "virtual" locations, etc. Once you've been labeled a spammer, you may find your listing removed or you may lose control of it. It's very difficult to get back into any directory's good graces after losing their trust.

Stay engaged and don't ignore communications

Many publishers try persistently to convert you to an upgraded (fee-based) listing, and you may find yourself developing a habit of automatically discarding their emails. But try to give them at least a quick skim before tossing them. For one thing, some enhancements may be worth your consideration. But more important, it's not unusual for an important update to be included in a message that appears to be pure marketing. (This is another good reason to divvy up directory monitoring duties among staff.)

Capko & Morgan worked with several private practices whose listings were consolidated under a hospital system umbrella on one of the physician ratings sites. Physicians' phone numbers were replaced by the hospital's call center, and the doctors' profiles were decorated with hospital branding. Although these physicians had staff privileges at the hospital, they were not employees—but the branding and centralized phone number gave patients the impression they were. Worst of all, the representatives at the central call center of the hospital were not instructed to direct patients who'd called in for a specific physician only to that physician; instead, they were sometimes diverting the calls to the hospital's employed doctors.

Not surprisingly, the practices don't believe they ever gave permission for this change. The directory maintains that the physicians were sent multiple notices of the plan to aggregate the listings under the hospital's brand, and that the physicians never indicated they wanted to be excluded. We can't know for sure what happened in that case, but it seems likely that emails about the switch were never seen or responded to by the practices involved. The case underscores the importance of keeping an eye on both your listings and messages from directories publishers.

Watch for duplicate listings

Be sure to request any duplicate listings be removed or merged into the proper listing as soon as you notice them. When more than one profile exists for a physician, reviews may be split between the two—meaning that some of your best reviews might wind up on a hidden or less prominent unclaimed profile.

CASE STUDY: Hospital learns the new basics of practice marketing

When Capko & Morgan met the doctors of "Friendly Family Practice,"[22] their business had been acquired a year before into the growing "Heavenly Hospital" network of primary care and cardiology practices. Prior to the acquisition, Friendly's enthusiastic and warm physicians had a history of high productivity, routinely hitting the 75th percentile or higher in national revenue benchmarks. This impressive performance was one reason Heavenly pursued them. Heavenly's ambitious financial projections for the acquisition also depended on Friendly's high productivity continuing.

The Friendly team was motivated to maintain their productivity, too. This was partly because they had agreed to a productivity-based compensation plan. But they were also proud of their practice's business success and roster of loyal patients. They looked forward to making their practice a great asset to Heavenly.

Everyone was on the same page. There was clear "hospital-physician alignment," as acquisition experts like to say. So ... what could go wrong?

Despite everyone's best intentions, a year post-acquisition, Friendly Family Practice's patient volume was only about a third of what it had been. Although Friendly's patients had been very loyal and happy, most of them had not followed to their new location (which was only about a mile away). New patients weren't coming in fast enough to make up much of the difference. In fact, new patients were barely trickling in at all.

Conflict brews as patient volume declines

Heavenly wondered if the doctors had been honest about the strength of their patient relationships. If Friendly's patients had been truly

---

[22]The names and identifying details have been changed in this case study, and quotes from the web paraphrased to anonymize the case.

satisfied, why weren't they still with the practice—especially since it now offered even more services in a beautiful new facility, just a stone's throw from their old office? It just didn't make sense that the patients would go elsewhere when the doctors they supposedly loved now offered them even more comfort and convenience.

The doctors were feeling equally let down by Heavenly. They thought that the hospital marketing director had failed to commit enough budget to their practice—even though Heavenly had spent thousands on bus side ads, Google ads, and a new family practice website. The doctors couldn't explain why their longstanding patients were defecting. But if Heavenly was advertising enough, shouldn't that have brought in new ones? Their community had fewer primary care doctors per capita than comparable areas, and the demographics were strong: low unemployment, growing local employers, and relatively high incomes. Friendly also offered a convenient, appealing whole-family primary care option to the young families in the area. Shouldn't new patients be flocking to the practice?

It was tough listening to both sides. It seemed clear to us that everyone had tried their best—and they were all taking the failure hard. Relationships were fraying due to stress and growing distrust. The hospital team was anxious, because Friendly Family Practice was draining cash, instead of contributing to profits. The smart, dedicated marketing director felt she had done all she could to promote the practice; there just wasn't more budget for further advertising. And the doctors were frustrated and discouraged. They felt that they had been set up to fail and betrayed.

If the trend couldn't be reversed, things would only get harder for everyone. Without enough patients, the doctors simply couldn't meet their productivity numbers. They would soon face a huge reduction in compensation. They'd then likely feel compelled to look for new employment, which would break up their tight-knit team. If the doctors left, the hospital would suffer greatly, too, with even less chance to recoup their investment in the acquisition.

A less-than-ideal transition

If this story sounds scary to you, it should. (It was scary to us.) The practice's decline was shockingly rapid. And enormous amounts of money and many careers were on the line.

It was critical to everyone that we figure out why the practice wasn't busier. Why weren't the doctors' prior patients still loyal to the practice? And why weren't new ones drawn to it?

To determine a solution, our first task was to learn why the hospital had decided to focus on outdoor advertising and pay-per-click. Normally, the first step in marketing a new practice with existing patients would be to contact the patient base directly. It turned out that the marketing director had faced a huge obstacle: She had no way to access Friendly's patient base.

Friendly had previously been owned by another hospital-based network, "Beachside Health." Friendly had never been an ideal fit in their network, so Beachside had been quite open to Friendly's plan to join Heavenly.

But that openness didn't translate to availability of medical and billing records. Whether it was because they weren't contractually required to do it or because their outdated systems wouldn't permit it, Beachside did not provide Friendly with access to any of their patients' records or even demographic information. Instead, Friendly and Heavenly had to fax a paper request to Beachside every time they wanted a medical record for an established Friendly patient.

This was a huge hassle for the practice and patients alike. Friendly had even had to add staff just to deal with the problem. Still more damaging, it meant that Friendly and Heavenly had no access to patients' email or postal addresses—so they had no way to proactively let them know about Friendly's physicians' new location.

This explained the bus advertising investment. We can't mail the patients, the marketing director reasoned, but perhaps by blanketing the community with ads featuring pictures of their doctors, we can get the word out around town that the doctors had moved. She also thought the campaign would do double duty in attracting prospective patients to Heavenly's new family practice. Prospective patients could also be reached with the pay-per-click ads on Google.

The bus sides seemed to be a cost-effective way to reach many local residents, including many existing patients. But as she talked through her strategy with us, we began to realize that there was another problem that the marketing director hadn't planned for—and it related directly to her experience as a hospital marketing professional.

Hospital marketing differs from physician marketing

Hospitals have different marketing needs than practices. They're large, visible, physical institutions in a community. They rarely change locations. It's unlikely that patients will ever have trouble finding them.

Physicians, on the other hand, can move around and be hard to find. Their contact information is critical to patients. It must be kept up to date. Patients also have more choices to make when it comes to physicians, so they tend to research them more than they might a hospital.

When they become interested in a doctor, whether because they saw an ad or received the name of a doctor from a friend or another physician, most patients check the doctor out on the internet. Some patients might want to know more about the doctor's reputation. Others just want key basics—like how convenient the office location is and whether the doctor is in their health plan network. And virtually every patient will need to look up a new doctor's contact information.

As we listened to the marketing director's strategy, we began to suspect that she hadn't included a plan to address patients' online research after seeing the bus ads—that is, to take charge of the practice's online reputation. And we suspected that this missing detail—which wouldn't have added much, if any money at all, to the budget—may have neutralized Heavenly's substantial marketing investment.

Following our hunch, we did a quick internet search on Friendly's doctors. Sure enough, it revealed many problems. Many prominent websites listed Friendly's physicians at their old address, with their now-disconnected old phone numbers. For example, the directory listings and maps on Google and Bing looked spiffy and credible, with current-looking photos of the doctors, website links, etc. But the links went to Beachside's site, and the addresses and phone numbers were wrong. Beachside even still listed the physicians on their own family practice page—also with the obsolete phone number.

SEO is not enough: the new normal

Heavenly had created a new family practice website within its web network, with all the information patients would need to find the doctors. They had been careful about SEO and assumed that patients would find the Heavenly site first when searching for the doctors online, especially since they were running pay-per-click ads. But patients weren't as likely see the doctors on the Heavenly site as they were on other web resources.

In the past, practice websites would often land on the top of search results, especially if their designers understood SEO. But because of the explosion of healthcare directories, this is now much less common. Top search slots are more typically filled with directory and reviews sites.

Additionally, many patients start with payer directories instead of a web search, to be sure the doctor they want to see participates in their plan. Our quick search of a few key payer sites revealed incorrect data for the Friendly docs there was well. The newest member of the physician team wasn't listed in a key plan's national directory at all.

Patients are vocal about administrative problems

Devastatingly, these errors had caused patients pain—and they let their feelings about it be known online. Complaints on sites like Yelp about Friendly's "inconsideration" in failing to notify patients about the move abounded. Some patients had made appointments months before the move, then missed them because they went to the wrong location—getting billed for a no-show fee on top of their troubles[23]. Some accused Friendly of "going corporate" and "selling out," even though the Beachside network they left was actually larger than the Heavenly group they joined.

Now when patients looked for the Friendly doctors online, they not only found inconsistent address and phone information, they also found negative reviews.

Little did either the marketing director or the practice administrator know what problems neglecting online directories would cause. Not only were previously happy patients switching doctors in frustration, Friendly's directory problems meant that prospective new patients were missed, too— and it wasn't just because they saw some of the negative reviews. Some op-

---

[23]Are you wondering why the practice administrator didn't arrange for patients to be reminded about the address change at the same time they were reminded about their appointments? We were, too. This was another failure in communication that shouldn't have happened. Providing patients with information like this right when they need it doesn't always seem like "marketing" —but not providing it surely results in the opposite of good marketing.

portunities were lost because of invalid phone numbers in payer directories. Some new patients would call the number next to a Friendly physician, but the phone would ring at Beachside—and the patient would be booked with a doctor there. Other patients whose plans didn't contract with Beachside were scared off when they stumbled upon the physicians' pictures on the Beachside site. (Friendly was actually able to accept many more new plans as part of the Heavenly network than it had as part of Beachside.)

Unaware of the importance of online physician profiles, the hospital's marketing director hadn't included a process for claiming and updating them into her marketing plan. While she was aware that patients might rate doctors online at reviews sites, the administrator had no idea how important the sites had become as resources for basic physician data. Adding to the problem, the practice administrator had also never learned about payer directory listings.

Despite seeing all the errors online, the hospital and the physicians were initially skeptical that simply fixing these free resources would get them back on track. But at our urging, they agreed to make fixing these problems a priority.

Time-consuming, but not difficult—and very valuable

The process took longer than it would have if Friendly had claimed their listings before their move. Dealing with some listings after a move, rather than in advance, can be a bureaucratic time sink. Google, for example, uses your currently listed phone number or address to validate your ownership of your listing. If you try to claim your listing after you've moved, the confirmation phone calls and postcards Google sends will be received by someone else (or no one at all). That can mean a long slog through Google's layers of staff to prove your practice has moved before they'll update the directory.

Although these types of problems made the process tedious for the marketing director and practice administrator, they worked together and eventually got the physicians' profiles cleaned up. It took a few months to get listing data corrected and to post responses owning the mistakes. They also had to persuade Beachside to remove the Friendly doctors from their site. But once the work was done, the payoff was dramatic.

When we spoke with the marketing director six months after our project, it was like talking to a new person. No longer discouraged and gloomy, she reported that the physicians were busy again. Their schedules were getting full, and they were even evaluating adding clinicians. Best of all, this progress was made without spending a penny more on marketing.

Not being able to reach out to patients directly was an unusual constraint for Friendly Family Practice and the marketing director at Heavenly Hospital. But by causing online directories to be neglected in favor of paid advertising, it provided us with a fascinating test case for how marketing programs and online directories need to sync up for good results. When directory data is wrong, it negates the impact of paid marketing. The dramatic impact of directory data on patient volume proves these basics should be the starting point of any practice marketing effort.

Top tips for expertly claiming and managing profile data

Know your market: search like a patient

Payer and hospital directories, search engines' own directories, and Healthgrades and Vitals are your first targets for reviewing, updating and expanding listing information. The sites you focus on next should be influenced by search rankings for your specialty in your local market.

Try the kind of searches your prospective patients are likely to try. See what Google and Bing return for results. Search on your name (and common misspellings of it), but not just your name—search on your specialty (and any plain-English variants, like "heart doctor" in place of cardiologist) and conditions (including alternatives–e.g., search on "maternity care" or "maternity doctor" and again on "pregnancy" with care, medicine, doctor, etc.). These exercises can help you see which sites tend to appear on top of search results for different searches patients will try. (While you're at it, make a note to include these phrases in your website's copy, to help your site move up in the results as well.)

Add details to stand out

Ensuring that basic data is correct, especially contact and specialty data, is the top priority. Adding a recent photo is next, then condition and procedure data that patients might search on. Don't miss a chance to be found by patients who are looking for exactly what your practice does. Some sites indicate whether a physician is accepting new patients. If you're accepting new patients, make sure your profile says so.

Explore bulk update and access options

Directories often have tools to enable one administrator to manage multiple listings more easily. Vitals allows users to manage up to 10 listings per registered user (admin or physician), and Google My Business has a handy tool that allows bulk uploading of up to ten addresses. Even if you don't see a link for bulk management, it may be possible to get multiple listings assigned to your account. (For example, Healthgrades offers assistance if you contact its customer service department.) If you've got a large number of listings to manage, ask what options are available.

Search—and monitor—for incorrect listings and new services

Make sure you catch all the outdated addresses, names, and phone numbers for your practice by searching on them. (E.g., go to Google and search on "fred darby md 423 main street danville CA"—with "423 main street" being the outdated address you're looking to scrub out.)

Once you've claimed and updated your listings, keep an eye on them. Set calendar reminders to check them at least annually (more frequently for the most important ones). Remember, reviews and ratings directories rely on public databases, and a faulty update to one of them could add incorrect information to your listing.

Setting up Google Alerts (www.google.com/alerts) for your practice and physicians' names is an easy way to be notified when new information is published about them. Setting up alerts for related subjects such as "healthcare price comparison" or "physician pricing" can help you learn of new companies that are publishing your details for patients.

Manage temp help actively

Hiring a temporary helper to work on your listings can be a time-saver, especially if your practice is very lean. But be sure the contractor or other helper only has control over the listings for as long as necessary to add or update the listings. A generic email address you control, such as info@ or listings@yourpracticedomain.com makes outsourcing cleaner, easier, and less risky. Change the password to listing accounts and to the email account once the helper no longer needs access.

Involve staff

Maintaining and polishing your listings can be a wonderful opportunity for internet-savvy staff to add skills while contributing meaningfully to practice growth. Claiming and updating listings can be done a little bit at a time, so it's also a great way to take advantage of occasional idle periods.

If you've never taken a look at any of your directory listings before, there will be quite a bit to do. Dividing the tasks up among staff can help you make a quick start. Getting everyone in on the project will make shorter work of it and create a sense of teamwork. Plus, fixing errors and enhancing your physicians' online profiles can increase new patient contacts quickly. Monitor new patient appointments to see if the team's efforts are paying off, and let them share in the victory.

Take advantage of updates and analytics

Led by Google's detailed dashboards, directory publishers are increasingly providing practices with access to data about how frequently their profiles are viewed and alerting profile administrators when new reviews are published.

Make sure that this information can get past the spam folder by adding the domain to your contacts or setting up a special filter. And make sure the emails come to the person best suited to monitor them and deal with issues—another good reason to be sure they're sent to an attended email address on your practice domain, even if an external party has helped you claim and polish your listings initially.

With the information we've covered so far in this section, you and your practice staff can begin taking control of your online reputation. Patient ratings and reviews are not likely to go away any time soon. High deductible plans and the constant change of healthcare reform are prompting patients to spend more time comparing and researching doctors. Stay engaged so you can learn and benefit from this growing online trend. The first step is to monitor and manage your online information.

Would you value a "cheatsheet" to help you organize your listings management process? Email me at info@capko.com and I'll send you one in Microsoft Word format.

You're listed ... now start listening

Once you've started managing your profile data, you're well on your way to managing your online reputation. Your next task is to maintain your connection with these sites to monitor, respond to, and benefit from the patient feedback they provide.

Keep reviews and ratings in perspective

If you've been hanging back because you've been imagining all kinds of horrible things misinformed patients could be saying online, data analysis has good news for you: most reviews are positive. Many respected researchers and organizations have analyzed physician reviews and ratings sites over the past several years, including the National Institutes of Health (NIH)[24], and the verdict seems consistent: most patients don't review their doctors, but among those that do, ***reviews tend to be positive.***

Patients don't expect perfection

Even though most reviews are positive, your practice is likely to get a bad review or two at some point—after all, nobody's perfect, not you, not your practice, and not the patients doing the reviewing. But keep in mind that patients don't expect perfection, either. A constructively worded negative review among mostly positive ones is unlikely to be weighted more heavily by patients. In fact, some people argue that a sprinkling of negative reviews among a majority of positive ones may even enhance the credibility of the profile, because a profile with just a few glowing reviews may appear to reflect only the opinions of a few close 'fans' of the practice.

---

[24] NIH research available here: http://www.ncbi.nlm.nih.gov/pubmed/23372115

So don't overreact to a few negative comments—take a deep breath, then determine if there is useful feedback that can help you improve your practice, and whether or not you should respond.

Negative reviews provide valuable learning opportunities

Many physicians question whether patients have the knowledge needed to rate their doctors, and, if you're among them, you might be pleasantly surprised to know that ratings sites typically emphasize many non-clinical criteria: scheduling, billing, wait times, office staff attitudes, etc. Patients aren't just qualified to rate your practice on these metrics, they're the best qualified to do so. Plus, *you need to know these opinions*. As a busy physician or manager, you already know that you can't personally observe every interaction between staff and patients or individually track every patient's progress through the practice. Patient reviews provide an opportunity—a priceless one, really—to learn about breakdowns in your systems that you might otherwise miss.

For example, a quick look at the patient satisfaction page for a physician listing on Healthgrades shows that there are several ratings specifically relate to the office and staff: ease of scheduling urgent appointments; office environment, cleanliness, etc.; staff friendliness and courteousness; and total wait time. Problems in these areas may not be apparent when everyone's working hard and the office is very busy. Honest feedback will help you fix problems that silently cut into practice profitability and efficiency. If you're using an outsourced billing service, you may feel especially in the dark about the service your patients are receiving—reviews can shed some much needed light on how your service is representing your practice.

Even ratings that aim to measure the clinical side usually focus on things that reflect a patient's personal experience—not clinical expertise per se. For example, Healthgrades asks the patient to rate how well the physician explained medical conditions; the amount of time spent on the visit; how well the physician listened and answered questions; and the patient's level of trust in the physician. It's beneficial for all clinicians to get a sense of how they're coming across to patients on these measures. Many patients are just too shy to bring up concerns about these interactions while inside the practice—and if they're really uncomfortable, they might just look for another physician instead.

Besides providing some insight into patient service, the responses to questions about the encounter may also reflect your effectiveness at promoting patient engagement. Some studies suggest that patients who have stronger ties to their physician and are more engaged in their own care have better outcomes. Better outcomes are a reward any practice will prize—but soon patient engagement may bring financial rewards as well, because payers have begun to credit engagement with lowering costs. The ability to make patients feel engaged is also a powerful way to bring new patients to your practice through referrals.

When and how to respond to reviews

When faced with a painful or particularly harsh review, it can be tempting to ask the publisher to take it down. But unless a negative review is demonstrably erroneous or fraudulent (i.e., written by a non-patient confused by a common last name, or containing false factual data), it's almost certain the publisher will not consider removing it. (Occasionally, a directory might allow suppression of a subset of reviews—Vitals, for example, allows physicians to suppress up to two—but this is not typical.) It's usually a waste of time to try to persuade a publisher to delete a review. So what should you do instead?

Truly fraudulent, vindictive reviews—e.g., posts by angry former employees or competing practices masquerading as patients—are fortunately rare. But most practices will receive at least a one or two valid negative reviews over time, especially very busy doctors who have lots of reviews. Besides learning from the content of reviews, it may be beneficial to your practice to respond. When and how you respond can make a big difference in the impression your profile makes on prospective patients.

First, do no harm

As of this writing, many directories, including Google and Healthgrades, only offer one option for responding to reviews: posting a response online. This means your response will become a permanent part of your profile, and it will be seen again and again by future visitors. In other words, when you publicly respond to a review, you're not just responding to the original poster, *you're responding to every future visitor of your profile*. Your public response can either help your cause or make a bad impression worse—so consider what your write carefully.

If feedback has upset you, it might be better to prepare your response after a cooling-off period. A response that is defensive or angry in tone will almost surely do more harm than good. (Imagine yourself as a reader checking out reviews of a local business. If you saw a negative review that contained potentially valid criticism, and the owner's reaction was simply to argue or deny the feedback, how might that affect your interest in supporting the business?) Keep in mind that readers of your profile will consider your responses to be an indication of your attitude towards patients.

If you feel you can't respond to a comment without arguing or losing your composure, it might be best not to respond at all. This is especially true if the review is the only negative one, or if there are only a few negative reviews among mostly positive reviews; if a review seems gratuitous or incorrect to you, and most other reviews have been positive, visitors may simply take the negative comments with a grain of salt as well.

Responding directly

In some cases, you might be able to contact a reviewer personally, as Yelp permits via its response system, and encourage the poster to contact you for a private conversation or meeting. Doing so can be a way to learn more about the patient's concerns, so that you can address them (for future patients, at least). But if you can't view such an interaction as an opportunity to learn or to make a bad situation right for a valued patient, think before getting in touch. Contesting the review is not likely to help (except, perhaps, in rare cases in which a reviewer mistook you for a different physician with a similar name—but even in those case, extend an olive branch and be respectful before launching into an argument).

Be careful about HIPAA and privacy

Before responding to any specific review, whether publicly or privately, remember that maintaining patient privacy (and complying with HIPAA) is mandatory. If a patient has posted a review that hints at (or even reveals) personal clinical information, reply that you'd like to speak with them by phone or in person in the office to both address their concerns and maintain their privacy.

Besides maintaining HIPAA compliance and protecting the patient from accidentally revealing private information, inviting the patient to call or come in reinforces your commitment to patient care and service. It's important, though, to monitor sites for new comments, so that you can follow up promptly—suggesting patients call to discuss a disappointing incident or misunderstanding will mean less if you do it long after the problem occurred.

Even if you're using a website's system for responding privately to a poster, encourage the reviewer to call you or visit before getting into a specific discussion. The reviews site is not a HIPAA business associate of your practice, and you have no guarantees of the security of the site's system for private communications. Always urge patients to call or come into the office, and leave specifics out of electronic communications.

When inviting patients to a conversation about the issue they're raising, be sure to indicate who they should ask for. If they experienced a billing, scheduling, or other business-related issue, they should be invited to speak with the practice administrator or manager. If the issue was clinical, urge them make an appointment to speak with the clinician or his or her supervisor—and make sure staff is alerted to reach out to help set a time on the appointment schedule and make sure the follow up happens.

Explain if you've addressed an issue

Sometimes, you know the reasons for a drop in survey results or a spate of negative reviews, and have since corrected them. For example, maybe you had a buggy phone system or answering service that you've since replaced, were short-staffed during a very busy period, or just know that service was unavoidably disrupted by a move or a distracting technology or billing service transition. Include a brief explanation of how you've upgraded patient service in your public response. You'll offset some of the earlier negative comments, and maybe even make them seem outdated, especially if they're followed by more recent comments that validate how much your service has improved.

If feedback from a ratings site helped you learn about problems patients experienced at your practice, and you've since corrected them, let people know. A general statement about how patient feedback helped you improve not only lets prospective patients know the problems are behind you, it also reinforces how much you care about the patient experience.

Acknowledge and thank

It's a nice idea to say thanks for feedback, even negative feedback that stings. It may seem odd to thank someone for negative comments. But the reviewer cared enough about the experience at your practice to write about it—acknowledge the effort and the fact that feedback helps you improve.

In some cases, your public response will be limited to a generalized response to all your reviews (Healthgrades, for example, mentions in its FAQ that you can do so through their customer service department); in others, you'll have the option to address reviews individually. When you're able to respond individually, make note of specific comments from the reviewer that have helped you improve your practice.

Should you respond to a positive review?

It's a nice idea to thank a patient that took the time to review your practice. But leave it at 'thanks,' and resist the temptation to ask that reviewer to send referrals or post elsewhere. And if the review was positive but wasn't perfect? Resist the temptation to nitpick, especially over details of a mostly-positive review. You'll likely seem ungrateful—and, a review with a little bit of balance to it is likely to be perceived as much more credible to a reader, anyhow.

Responding to a personal attack—or a review that's just wrong

While thankfully rare, you may be unlucky enough to experience a review posted by a person with an axe to grind, and that review may even contain personal attacks and comments you believe are simply untrue.

If you feel that there is information in the review that identifies it as fraudulent, it may be useful to point this out to the site publisher. Publishers generally don't have an interest in promoting inaccurate or faked reviews—typically they even have their own algorithms to exclude reviews that contain suspicious sounding language, such as an excess of medical terminology (suggesting the review was not posted by a layperson). If a review wasn't caught by the publisher's filter, but you still have evidence that it's fake or a mistake, it makes sense to point this out.

Examples of indicators of suspicious or mistaken reviews include:

- Mentions services you don't offer or unrelated to your specialty
- Refers to a location in which your practice has no office or presence
- Too clinical: sounds like it was written by a clinician and not a patient
- Mentions a clinician who isn't part of your practice or has since left
- Misspelling of physician or NPP name in text, or other indication the patient selected the wrong listing to post to
- Overly or oddly specific examples
- Doesn't describe patient's own, individual experience—speaks for another person or in generalities
- Other patterns inconsistent with your practice specialty or services

Any of these things may be enough information for the site to reconsider publishing the review. If a review reveals any confidential information, that's also usually reason enough to persuade a reviews site to block or remove the review. Bring these issues to the attention of the reviews sites through their contact pages (usually, you're looking for 'support'—with an email like support@vitals.com) or by flagging the review (done from within the review itself using a flag button or link).

If you're convinced the review really isn't from one of your patients, but the site doesn't agree, you could post a reply with a message such as, "Some of the information you shared sounds like it might refer to another practice. But if there's any chance you were our patient, we want to know more about what happened so that we can improve and correct our mistakes. Please call our office and ask for our manager so that figure out what went wrong while maintaining your privacy." Remember HIPAA at all times—don't call out specific clinical information, even if the reviewer did in their comments. And if you decide to respond, remember that whatever you publish will remain on your profile indefinitely. (Remember also that not responding may be best. If you feel a review is clearly not about your practice and its negative tone is out-of-step with the others, visitors to your profile will probably recognize it as a mistake as well and discount it.)

If you believe a review was meant for your practice but find it to be unfairly harsh, use caution when responding, especially if you're upset. You don't want to appear defensive, and you don't want to lower yourself to the standards of an unfair attack. Perhaps you can salvage the relationship with a light touch. Consider responding with a simple message encouraging the poster to call your office as soon as convenient. Sometimes, a person who was enraged because he thought his needs were ignored while in your office may begin to reconsider simply because you reached out. Both patients and practices have off days—especially in our field, where any 'customer' could be feeling very ill, troubled by an unfavorable diagnosis, or in pain. Prospective patients may recognize this, too, and a review that's really inconsistent with the other comments will likely be given less weight.

Support your staff

Staff members often take the brunt of criticism in online reviews. Sometimes, reviews reveal that some staff members are insufficiently trained or not well-suited to their roles. Other times, staff may be doing their best possible job, but systems may be letting them down, and patients who can't tell the difference lash out at employees in their reviews.

Whether employees are making avoidable mistakes or systemic problems are to blame, remember that being called out on a reviews site for criticism can be just as painful for staff members as it is for you. They may feel even worse about it than you do if they perceive that there's nothing they can do about the things they're criticized for.

When feedback on reviews sites prompts you to look at staff performance and your workflow for improvements, do so sensitively. Allow staff to make suggestions to address problems and improve service.

DOs: Smart ways to improve ratings

Over the long haul, the best way to deal with an occasional negative review is to make sure it's a rarity. Learn from constructive criticism, of course, but then be sure to invite all of your patients to add their reviews, so that the (hopefully happy) majority can share their experiences. Here are some patient-friendly ways to shift the ratings balance in your favor:

Survey patients yourself

One way to head off negative reviews on the web is to ask patients for feedback yourself. Many times, just being asked conveys to patients that you care about their view and boosts their opinion of your practice. You may also learn about problems with scheduling, wait times, and other issues more quickly this way, so that you can nip them in the bud before they affect other patients.

When a patient seems upset about something that occurred during their visit—whether a long wait, a missed prescription refill request, or other problem—a quick intervention by the manager *before* the patient leaves the office can help a lot. If you know what happened, apologize and reassure the patient you're either working on fixing your processes or that the situation was unusual and it won't happen again. If you don't know why a patient seems upset, ask if there was anything your practice could have done better. Make sure all patients can easily find out how to speak with your manager if they have a concern.

Investing in ongoing surveys is another way to learn what patients really think—to both learn about issues you need to address and give your patients a forum to express opinions without publicizing them. Be sure to allow patients to give their feedback anonymously. While you may find it expedient to do-it-yourself (for example, using Survey Monkey), third-party management of patient surveys can reduce the burden on your staff and give you more confidence that you've reached a representative sample. (Plus you'll be able to work with a survey writer who has experience designing clear and unbiased questions.) Check to see if your specialty society or management organization can help with recommendations, or perhaps has partnered with a firm that offer a discount on services to members.

Collect emails

The ability to solicit feedback easily is one more reason to collect emails on your face sheets. Be sure to ask patients for permission to send them non-clinical email, so that you can invite them to a survey or to post a review on a ratings site. Including your requests in a newsletter with other information for patients—announcements, such as flu shot clinics, new physicians or other practitioners, or back-to-school services; healthy recipes; your practice's participation in local events; classes; etc. This way, your patients won't feel the email was purely promotional, and so may be more inclined to make the effort to write a review.

Encourage reviews on ratings sites

Many practices have found that simply reminding patients at the front desk can help build reviews. Some sites offer marketing materials to help, such as the "Find us on Yelp" window stickers that are available for free from Yelp. You can also put reminders and web addresses on the back of appointment cards. Avoid being too pushy; remind your patients that you're profiled on reviews sites, but allow them to decide whether to review you without feeling pressured.

To maximize the benefit of your review-boosting efforts, don't spread them too thin. Focus on one or two reviews sites where you already have a presence and which appear prominently in search results.

Use reputation management software to add reviews

Besides helping you to efficiently manage multiple directory listings from a single dashboard, reputation management software makes it easy for staff to request reviews from patients after they receive services. The software is usually integrated with your PMS, so staff can easily select patients and seamlessly email them to request a review. Plus, you can decide which reviews site you'd prefer to direct patients to—handy for quickly building a base of reviews on a visible site.

Besides making it easy to request reviews on sites you prefer, using reputation management software allows you to target actual patients of your practice. Because the process is fast and easy, you'll be able to make the requests soon after the patient visits—when they'll be more likely to remember the experience and be willing to post.

Use a kiosk or tablet (or two) in reception

Some practices have found that one way to get more reviews is to make it easy for patients to write them before they leave your practice. A computer kiosk or tablet(s) for this purpose makes it easy for patients to log in before they leave, with links on the home screen to their preferred reviews sites. But if you try this approach, be sure not to pressure patients to complete reviews before they leave. If patients feel a "hard sell," they might respond with negativity in their review. Some directory sites also monitor the IP addresses that reviews come from—and discount or exclude multiple reviews from a single location, which may invalidate your efforts.

Making web access available for patients to use before or after their visit can contribute to other important goals besides generating reviews. Many practices are looking for ways to help patients become more comfortable using their portals. So instead of focusing on getting reviews from patients, you might try inviting patients to test their portal logins and sending their physician a message before they leave the practice. After patients log out of their trial of the portal, a home screen with links to your preferred reviews sites and a message inviting them to make a quick rating can be a softer way to encourage reviews.

DON'Ts: Resist methods that do more harm than good

Don't encourage reviews from non-patients

If asking patients to write reviews is good … would asking all your friends and family be better? And why not hire someone to just create reviews for your practice? These tactics might seem like an easy way to goose your online ratings, but don't be tempted. It's not only dishonest, it's considered a new form of false advertising called 'astroturfing,' and it's illegal—and the penalties can be severe. Plastic surgery marketer Lifestyle Lift paid $300,000 to settle its astroturfing case with the New York attorney general[25]; the damage to its reputation probably greatly exceeded that figure.

Don't target a few patients or 'reward' them

Just as fake reviews from non-patients constitute false advertising, it's illegal to compensate *anyone* to write a positive review—even a genuine patient, and even if the review reflects their true opinion.

---

[25] See: http://www.ag.ny.gov/press-release/attorney-general-cuomo-secures-settlement-plastic-surgery-franchise-flooded-internet

Some practices have tried targeting the happiest patients in the office to request they post a review. But this is also risky, because it could be observed by other patients who will wonder why you're not asking them to post a review. Keep your review-promoting efforts simple and transparent—and trust that most patients want to support their physicians.

Don't attempt to silence patients

A few years ago, some firms began offering reputation management services that included contracts for patients to sign that forbid reviewing their doctor, transferred the copyright of patient reviews to the doctor, or otherwise attempted to contractually restrict patients from reviewing the services they received. Some clinicians who bought in found themselves in much more trouble than a few bad reviews would have caused them.

In one famous case, a dentist used a contract to attempt to restrict patients' rights to rate her online; when one patient ignored the contract and posted a negative review, the dentist tried to enforce the contract. The case received national attention—very negative attention for the dentist—and the patient prevailed when the contract was deemed illegal.

Even if there weren't the risk of a terrible blow-up like that dentist experienced, and even if 'gag contracts' that attempt to curtail patient ratings weren't widely considered illegal, aiming to forbid patients from rating your practice would still be a terrible idea.

What kind of message would it send if, say, you brought your car in to be repaired and the shop demanded such an agreement? What if a financial advisor wanted to prevent you from telling others about your experiences with her service? Would you assume that these vendors provide the very best service—or that they believe you're likely to want to write a poor review? Attempting to silence or discourage reviews suggests that you're not confident your service that will stand up to review.

Don't buy incredible reputation management claims

Despite the debunking of things like gag contracts, some reputation management firms still make grandiose promises—including promising to remove negative reviews from ratings sites. But reputation management firms don't control reviews sites, their owners do. If you're offered a 'guarantee' that negative feedback will be expunged, be very skeptical. And if a firm promises to outweigh negative reviews with huge numbers of positive reviews, be absolutely sure you know how they'll do it—and that their approach is not unethical or even illegal.

Don't rush to sue

A painful negative review may make you want to grab the phone and call your lawyer, but defamation is difficult to prove. Patients are entitled to share their opinions. Trying to prove a review unfairly interfered with your practice business is very tough—and the effort could prove expensive. If you lose, you might even be on the hook for the patient's legal fees.

Remember, above all, a single review that seems so unfair that it makes you want to sue will also likely seem anomalous to people reading it, especially if it sits among many positive comments. If you take a patient to court, though, and the suit gets media attention, that could negatively impact your reputation much more than the original review.

PART FIVE

Less Work, More Money: Tech Secrets for Practice Profitability

Are you a technology skeptic? Maybe even a technology cynic? If you are, you're hardly alone among physicians and practice managers.

Many of the people my partners and I meet in our consulting work are dubious about the promises made by technology vendors. Many have been disappointed by, even seen their practices disrupted by, big technology investments, especially in EHRs. The fact that EHRs have so often seemed more focused on government goals than practice needs only rubs salt in the wound.

But all technology is not created equal. The market for medical front office technology is blooming with promising innovation—innovation that is focused on practice needs, not the government's priorities.

Theses solutions are often priced well and easy to deploy. Best of all, they make labor-intensive practice management tasks a whole lot easier.

Why this wave is different

I can almost hear you protesting, "But things are working fine in our practice. Why would I want to take another leap of faith on technology and risk another disruption? Will we be pouring more money down the drain?"

These are sensible questions to ask, even if you aren't still aggravated by a painful recent EHR or PMS conversion.

But because of how they function in a practice, EHRs and PMSs stand out as much harder and riskier to implement than other technologies. If you estimate how difficult or disruptive other solutions will be to implement based on your EHR experience, you'll likely be far too cautious.

As platforms, EHRs and PMSs are the main hub systems of your practice. They are comprehensive repositories of all of your data—medical records in your EHR, and billing and other practice management data in your PMS. The huge numbers of records and data fields these systems manage make implementing one (or switching) a very big deal.

Because they act as the central technology 'brain' for either the clinical or the revenue cycle workflow of your practice, you use only one of each of these systems. Choosing a new platform can feel perilous given the huge costs and hassles of switching, the need to standardize on one system, and the risk of even more problems if the system doesn't work as promised.

The latest front office tools, on the other hand, share none of these challenging traits. These solutions are more like spokes that plug into your hubs. They're focused applications that run on top of your PMS or EHR (like an app runs on your phone), or sometimes devices that connect with one of those platforms to exchange information.

These solutions don't need to host the data that an EHR or PMS contains; they simply connect to those systems to use (and sometimes update) their data. No complicated conversions are needed. You won't have to shut down your office to add, say, a check-in tablet, payment portal, or online scheduling solution. In fact, it's often feasible to get staff up and running on these products within hours—sometimes in minutes.

Because these products must play nicely with others to gain market acceptance, they're also less risky to try. They're designed to work with lots of different platforms. That means you'll often have multiple competitors to choose from for any solution—and you can also implement solutions from more than one vendor if your set-up requires it.

The pricing usually reflects a narrow focus, too. They're generally relatively inexpensive, and their ROI is usually easy to calculate. And in many cases, you'll simply swap one cost for another, such as with payment portals that process credit cards and charge a fee similar to what you'd pay a processor for swiping.

Most important, they address problems and inefficiencies that are difficult, if not impossible, to improve without technology. Even the most creative managers will eventually hit a process improvement wall: At some point, significant improvements can no longer be made by tweaking workflow rules, redefining jobs, or adding staff. When that limit is reached, technology is the only way to make a significant improvement to a labor-intensive process.

CASE STUDY: An overnight success, 18 years in the making

Mid-South Pulmonary Specialists, a 20-physician practice in Memphis, TN, has had its fair share of technology trials and tribulations. But the practice never allows the frustrations of failed initiatives to defeat its determination to use technology where it can do the most good. The practice's management team is always looking for innovative, proactive ways to use technology to correct inefficiencies that create extra work and undermine practice profitability.

One such problem had bothered Kim Avery, the practice's administrator, and her colleague Teresa Golden, practice manager, for nearly two decades before they found the right solution. It's a serious challenge that is common when physicians need to work in more than one place: capturing charges remotely.

Mid-South's physicians spend as much as 70% of their work hours at one of the seven hospitals the practice contracts with; only 30% of their time is spent seeing patients in their own clinic. In fact, most of the patients the practice sees in the clinic were first treated by their physician in a hospital. It's no exaggeration to say that the practice's profitability depends on accurately capturing charge data for hospital services and transmitting it promptly to the billing team.

Capturing and sending charge data is a task that cries out for automation. Speed and accuracy are critical. Manually documenting absorbs countless hours of valuable physician time—delaying processing and cutting into physician free time. Plus, once billing receives a physician's documentation, it must then be entered into the PMS—a wasteful duplication of effort that invites errors.

Yet despite the obvious market need for a solution, when Kim and Teresa began their quest for remote charge capture software in the late 1990s, no good option existed.

The physicians instead carried paper rounding lists to document charges for each of the 25-30 patients they'd see during a day in the hospital. The tedious task of writing up and faxing the charges to the office would typically take the doctors one to two hours at the end of a busy shift.

Kim and Teresa made many attempts to streamline the process, but inefficiencies and hassles persisted. For example, the doctors had no way to quickly look up codes while remote. Teresa and Kim came up with the idea of reference cards the doctors could carry with them that listed the practice's 100 most commonly used ICD and CPT codes. These aids helped with the bulk of the coding, but when a patient had an unusual diagnosis, the physicians transmitted their notes without codes. The billers then often struggled to determine the doctors' intentions, which led to time-consuming back-and-forth communications.

Working on paper caused other problems that were hard to avoid. Sometimes pages or entire faxes would go missing, creating more work for everyone; billers spent time chasing down missing documents, and doctors often wound up having to rewrite their charge slips. Billers also sometimes noticed that charges were missing for some patients, or had difficulty reading the physicians' handwriting. If the physician they needed clarifications from was off or on vacation, questions like these could add days to the billing process.

All of these inefficiencies carried costs. Teresa and Kim estimated that their normal lag between providing services and billing charges was seven to ten days—far from ideal. When faxes went missing or patient charges were inadvertently omitted from the physicians' paper forms, some of those charges were unrecoverable. And all the handling, monitoring, and research of charges meant that the billing department needed four full-time employees just to manage hospital charges.

Jumping onto the bleeding edge

No wonder Kim and Teresa were so determined to find an automated solution. But when they started their journey, smartphones and apps were far from pervasive. The internet revolution was still young. Remote access was gaining ground as an everyday business technology solution, but it was still considered leading edge (and sometimes "bleeding" edge). Organizations that wanted to automate using the internet often had to accept that the speed and efficiency they gained would likely be traded off with a risk of less-than-perfect reliability.

Teresa and Kim understood this risk, but they knew that *not* automating also carried significant risk: The practice was losing revenue every day because the paper-based workflow would never approach 100% accuracy. Automating the charge capture process would be the first step towards realizing more earned revenue. It was worth trying, even if the road would be bumpy at first. Progress they made towards automating the process would be a foundation they could continuously improve upon.

With this in mind, Kim and Teresa began searching for options. After several years, they found an opportunity that looked like a fit. In 2001, they decided to become a beta site for a Palm Pilot-based software product that didn't yet fulfill all their requirements, but came close. By working with beta software, they'd have the attention of the developers, and could potentially influence the development of the product. As they began, the limitations of the platform and the network technology of the era caused the most frustrations. The battery life of the handheld devices was too short; the doctors had to find opportunities to recharge during the day (and plan ahead to do so); and syncing the data on the device with their office computers meant tracking down an internet connection—something that was often easier said than done in hospitals in the early 2000s.

Gradually, the Mid-South team and the developers worked through many of the issues, finding solutions either through upgrades to the technology or adjustments to workflow. But just when the most important problems appeared to be addressed, the software company was acquired— and the new owner decided the product was not worth further investment. The search for a remote charge capture solution was back at square one.

Keeping their eyes on the prize

After the lengthy, arduous beta process ended with such disappointment, it would have been understandable if Kim and Teresa had decided to set their automation goal aside for a time. But these managers were far too experienced with technology to abandon their goal because of a single misstep, even an especially painful one. They knew that once they found the right solution, the return on investment would be significant. Besides the financial upside, a technology-enabled workflow would mean less stress for the entire team, especially for the doctors.

Happily, the technology market's evolution was accelerating. Internet infrastructure was improving dramatically. More doctors were using smartphones, and tablets were around the bend. These innovations, in turn, paved the way for better software. New entrants were coming up with better ways to solve remote access problems. The options were expanding.

What's more, the team had learned a lot from both their beta experience and their research of alternatives. They could be pickier about the next platform they selected because there would be more choices. Most important, their experience gave them a better sense of what they should be picky about.

Learning, applied: Focus on ROI

For the next few years, Teresa and Kim looked at many options and even tried building their own data capture approach. The process was at times discouraging, but it helped them home in on both "must have" attributes and deal-breakers.

For example, they noticed that many of the vendors focused their development on the front end of their solutions—i.e., the interface that physicians would use to enter their charges while out of the office. Perhaps they did so thinking that because the physician is usually the decision-maker, an impressive front end could be a shortcut to physician wallets. Certainly, a "sexy" interface for physicians helped sales people close deals. But focusing only on the front end left the biggest potential drivers of ROI—the hassles, duplicate efforts, and lost charges in the billing department—unaddressed. When Kim and Teresa talked directly with the sales reps' clients, they learned that many were ultimately disappointed. Usually, staff would still need to download and print the charges from a website; redundant data entry would still create many opportunities for errors and confusion, and the billing department workload would barely be reduced at all. Some of the practices that had purchased these solutions told Teresa and Kim that they'd stopped using the software because the process was actually worse than before for the billing team.

The Mid-South management team had also already tried developing a solution of their own that was easier for the physicians, but didn't integrate with their billing system. Through careful analysis of that experience, they learned that there would be no increase in practice profitability unless they found a way to integrate with the billing system on the back end. Now they also had data from actual clients of companies they were considering buying software from, and that data proved the same thing. A system that didn't just simplify the process for physicians, but also transmitted charge data directly to the practice's PMS, was a must.

As they considered emerging options, Kim and Teresa knew they needed to see how the software functioned through entire workflow of a real client practice. They developed a clear list of priorities any candidate worth considering would have to meet, which were:

- A handheld-device-based interface that would allow the physicians to look up and enter charges, meeting the physicians' expectations for utility and convenience;

- Integration with the practice's billing system/PMS;

- Integration with, or ability to build an interface with, the practice's EHR;

- Opportunity to observe the system in action at a current client practice—with views of every step of the process;

- Positive ROI when accounting for all costs including software, hardware, training, development, and support.

A candidate emerges

A company called pMD eventually hit Teresa and Kim's radar. Its software had recently been adopted by a gastroenterology practice whose physicians worked at some of the same hospitals as Mid-South's doctors. The physicians were able to see how their GI colleagues used the remote charge entry while in the hospital, and they liked what they saw. Kim and Teresa were able to get an end-to-end demonstration of the product from a practice that was actually using it. Besides seeing how the product could function within their own workflow, Kim, Teresa, and their team also learned about the snags the GI practice had encountered. This was information they could use to avoid the same problems if they moved ahead.

The pMD product looked like a winner. The team next spoke to their EHR/PMS vendor, NextGen, and learned that they would need to build a custom interface to pMD. But they also learned that pMD had already established a relationship with NextGen, which would make the integration process easier. The practice then secured a commitment from pMD to provide implementation help all the way through to a successful roll-out. The remaining step was to determine the ROI required to offset the cost of implementing and using pMD. After investing many hours in carefully calculating both the initial and ongoing costs, Kim and Teresa determined that the software would break even if it enabled the practice to eventually reduce billing headcount by two full-time equivalent (FTE) employees. Once they felt confident that pMD would eventually permit them to trim hospital billing staff by two, pMD was a go.

Planning for a successful implementation

A software product that will affect multiple stages of a critical practice workflow requires careful implementation planning. Any hiccup in the information flow could lead to errors or omissions that would repeat themselves every day; such errors could cause silent financial losses. Teresa and Kim were therefore very careful to set up a conservative roll-out process, to be sure the system was working exactly as expected before converting the entire charge capture process to pMD.

Their biggest concern was the potential for charges to "disappear," with no audit trail to find them. What would happen if the doctors entered their charges on their devices, transmitted them, but some of the information failed to land in the billing system? To test the system's reliability, the physicians used it for two weeks in parallel with their paper system. The physicians required some persuading to do double-entry during the test period, but Kim and Teresa presented a clear explanation of the pitfalls they were testing for, and why the test was so important. After the two weeks of testing showed that the billing system, the handhelds, and the paper charge slips all agreed, the team was finally ready to flip the switch.

The post-conversion results: happy doctors and faster, more accurate billing. Teresa and Kim's ROI target of two fewer billing staff was eventually met through attrition. But besides cost savings, the new system helps the practice bring in cash much more quickly (no more 10-day lags for routine billing), and fewer charges are missed. The physicians are happier that they can be more productive, and they're delighted that documenting charges is so much easier. One doctor even said, "pMD has changed my life. I don't have to spend two hours every day writing down charges anymore." Although the entire journey took nearly 20 years, the end result was even more transformative than the team had hoped.

Takeaways from the Mid-South case

Many independent practices are slower to act on technology than Mid-South Pulmonary Specialists. Many would shy away from being among the first to try new software, especially for critical workflows. But Mid-South is a good example of a practice that embraces technology, even sometimes technology that is not fully ready for prime time, because they see it as a key tool to help keep their practice strong and independent. They realize that technology is often the surest way to make a big step forward in efficiency—which can then bring improvements in both profitability and physician satisfaction. Being open to technology, even when there is a risk of failure, also helps them stay ahead of the curve, so that they can be even savvier about each successive investment.

Over more than 20 years of experimentation with practice management technologies, Mid-South has several principles that help guide their tech strategy, including:

- *Some processes will never be manageable without a technology solution.* Where no off-the-shelf software exists to fill a clear and critical need, it may make sense to experiment with being a beta site or even trying to develop your own software. A key part of Mid-South's strategy for growth and independence is serving many area hospitals. This would be much more difficult to do profitably without a reliable, efficient approach to remote charge capture. The importance of finding a tech solution that would help support the practice's overall strategy, plus the toll that paper processing was taking on the physicians, argued for taking a bit more risk than they might have if the upside hadn't been so significant.
- *Failures=learning opportunities.* The road to where you want to go may be bumpy, especially when you're an early adopter. But technology failures are usually valuable learning opportunities. Trying

and exploring so many different technical approaches to their charge capture problem made it much easier for Mid-South to eventually choose the right tech partner—and to complete a relatively hassle-free implementation.

- *Always get the whole picture.* Sales presentations and early editions of software often focus mainly on what physicians will want to see. Vendors hope to dazzle the players holding the purse strings with features that will appeal specifically to them. But if a technology touches multiple parts of the workflow, it's imperative to validate how it works for everyone who'll be using it.

- *View software in action at a real practice if possible.* If this isn't possible because you'll be an early adopter, get a free trial, customizations, or other compensation for the extra degree of difficulty and risk you'll be taking on.

- *Be disciplined about decision-making.* Mid-South relies on a somewhat formal process for embarking on large technology project or other major initiatives. When Kim and Teresa want to move ahead with an idea that requires physician approval and buy-in, they make a detailed presentation to the entire physician team. All stakeholders are encouraged to "kick the tires" and air their questions and concerns. The process keeps Teresa and Kim on their toes, since every initiative presented will be vetted by everyone for ROI and potential pitfalls before approval. It also ensures they have the buy-in they need to complete projects, even when roll-out temporarily increases everyone's workload.

- *Capture all the details that determine ROI.* Determining the ROI required for a project to "pencil out" takes time and focus. On the investment side, be sure not to overlook ongoing costs like upgrades, license fees, support, or hardware. And on the return side, try to capture not just hard costs avoided, but the financial impact of reduced errors and higher productivity.

- *Get your roll-out right.* Beta products and early-stage solutions are special cases. You know going in that you'll need to tolerate more problems. But when you're buying a packaged solution from an established vendor, you should be able to plan for a roll-out with minimal disruption. Be sure you know what parts of the system must be thoroughly tested before you can 'go live' and give your final approval of the implementation to the vendor. And be sure to secure the vendor's commitment to provide all the support you need (in person, if necessary) during your set-up and beyond.

Better software may be right under your nose

Mid-South Pulmonary knew what process they most needed to automate, and they set out to find the right technology—even before they knew if the market would be able to meet their needs. But the pace of front office technology innovation in recent years has been so brisk, proven solutions already exist that can improve accuracy and efficiency in most parts of the workflow.

Some of the very best, easiest-to-use tools may even be available to you without any shopping or implementation at all. As more EHR and PMS vendors have moved to the cloud, they've been able to roll out new features more quickly. Sometimes the speed of updates and upgrades means that important ones are easily overlooked. Features like real-time eligibility checking, payment portals, digital appointment reminders, waiting lists, and other valuable tools may already be available to you with the flip of a switch in your current set-up—as another client of ours was delighted to discover.

Laurie Morgan

CASE STUDY: Technology helps restore practice profitability, gets collections moving[26]

About a year ago, my partners and I worked with a primary care practice whose deep financial problems had suddenly come to a dramatic head. To paraphrase the apt old saying, this practice had gotten into trouble slowly—almost imperceptibly—then all at once.

While their problems were suddenly urgent, they were actually the cumulative effect of small unresolved issues over many years. Most frustratingly, the practice had many advantages, but some of those strengths had actually metamorphosed into liabilities.

For example, the practice was located in an affluent area and had a base of longstanding, chronically ill patients that visited regularly. Their patients were mostly well-insured and inclined to refer others. But these same well-off, well-connected patients had come to expect preferential treatment, the cost of which was catching up with the practice.

Long-established patients habitually requested, and expected, copay waivers. Without fully appreciating the financial impact[27], the well-meaning physician-owner had generally complied. Not surprisingly, this pattern was highly contagious. New patients checking in would observe others avoiding copayments and expect equal treatment. Staff tried their best to collect, but patients became more brazen and demanding over time, insisting the owner be summoned when they were asked to pay.

---

[26] A version of this case study was originally published © Medical Product Guide. Content reused with permission.

[27] We also advised the physician that he could be violating his payer contracts, since collecting copays at the time of service is commonly required, even though this may not have been the case with every plan he signed on with years before.

180

When the custom of waiving first took root, copays were only $5 or $10. The practice was brand new, and the owner (then a solo physician) was reluctant to upset patients over a trivial fee. But over the course of 15 years, health plan payment terms evolved dramatically. Copays can constitute as much as 25-35% of office visit revenue. Waiving them routinely had become a big drain on our client practice's revenue.

Many patients now also have deductibles that apply to office visits. But our client's patients were even less likely to pay those amounts at the time of service. Worried about angering patients, staff didn't try to collect or even explain that money was due. Patients were instead billed in full after insurance claims were processed, usually weeks later. Many patients called staff to complain about being surprised by "incorrect" bills. Others simply ignored the bills, month after month. Worst of all, some patients who stubbornly expected all charges to be waived became huffy and left the practice.

By the time we were brought in to help, the practice had a huge accumulation of patient receivables—hundreds of thousands of dollars per billing clinician, much of it uncollectable. The trend of health plans shifting payment responsibility to patients, combined with the practice's ineffectiveness at collecting, had finally pushed the practice to the financial brink.

A new manager, a new chapter

Fortunately, the practice was able to hire a skilled, motivated manager who joined soon after we began our engagement. The manager understood where the financial problems began: at the front desk, where collections efforts were rare; and in scheduling, where patients were not being alerted to their financial obligations. He knew that the practice needed to educate patients about insurance terms and change their expectations about paying. Our joint challenge was to figure out how to do this without alienating patients in the process.

We all believed that a first, crucial step was to help long-term patients understand that their payment responsibilities were set by their health plans, not by the practice. This needed to be done in a way that did not feel confrontational or embarrassing to patients. Collections at the front desk also had to be depersonalized, because feeling valued and "special" had become connected to copay "consideration."

The front desk staff understood how important it would be to make changes. But they were still nervous. They knew patients felt entitled to refuse to pay. The staff felt that they'd need very detailed, clear, reliable payment information at their fingertips—the missing piece of the puzzle that technology could provide. And the team also knew they'd need thorough preparation for explaining new rules to patients in a palatable way.

Tapping into technology already in-house

We all agreed that technology could play a critical role. The manager decided to first contact the practice's platform vendors, to learn if there were advanced features the practice wasn't using. We've worked with many practices that had missed out on helpful features because no one was in charge of tracking system alerts—or because updates were so frequent that important ones were easily missed.

Sure enough, the practice was underutilizing technology it already owned. For example, the PMS included a payment portal and email statements—features that were essentially free and could be launched immediately. The vendor would collect a fee for processing credit card payments through the portal; however, the amount of this fee was similar to what the practice paid its primary credit card service. The credit card expense was close to a wash, but the practice would see positive return by getting paid faster. Plus, total expenses for mailing statements, chasing payments by phone, and handling checks would be greatly reduced.

Once the decision was made, the practice enabled these tools in an afternoon, and received its first payments via the portal the same night. The manager and the practice owner were thrilled to see money in the bank the morning after turning on the portal!

Patients seemed pleased, too. They could now use the portal to make partial payments on balances due, without being embarrassed by having to admit in person or on the phone that they couldn't pay in full. Privacy was a big issue for the practice's image-conscious patient base, many of whom had surprisingly large balances despite their affluent lifestyles. With email statements, staff could also immediately send a fresh statement any time a patient wanted one.

The manager also learned that the practice's integrated EHR offered customizable digital and voice appointment reminders. He immediately implemented these, adding greetings that alerted patients about paying co-payments at check-in and encouraged them to check with their plans if they were unclear about payment obligations. This helped reinforce the idea that payment rules were set by their insurers, while also reducing the no-show/late cancel rate. Patients were delighted to try out the new reminder options: Many strongly preferred to be notified by text or email rather than a phone call.

The scheduling team also got a welcome technology surprise: real-time insurance verification from within the PMS. This new tool would eliminate a lot of manual steps and guesswork. The schedulers estimated that about 80% of the practice's payers would provide verification information and even copay and deductible amounts electronically. They saw immediately how it could help them be much clearer with patients about the precise terms of their plans and their payment responsibilities.

The schedulers worked up rough scripts to explain that terms are dictated by health plans, and define what copays and deductibles were for patients who'd never paid them before. For example, schedulers could say, "I'm contacting your health plan, now, Mrs. Jones. It will take just a moment. Yes, I see your plan has confirmed you're eligible. They've also said we're required to collect your $40 office visit copay at the time of service."

Enhancing front-desk collections—and privacy

Just taking advantage of the PMS and EHR features they'd been unaware of helped the practice accelerate patient payments. Staff felt much more confident and empowered to collect from patients going forward.

With the positive momentum gained from tapping into technology, the manager was ready to look at add-on solutions keep the trend going. We decided that the next step should be to bring automation to the front desk with a tablet system for check-in and copay collection.

Instead of entering patients' check-in data to the PMS, receptionists would now hand patients a tablet to check themselves in. Staff would add that "the tablet contacts your insurance company to determine your copay, and then you can swipe your credit card to pay."

Besides reinforcing the message about payment terms being set by health plans, the tablets offered patients more privacy in dealing with both payments and their health information. Patients were impressed and grateful that they could enter information like the reason for their visit confidentially into the tablet, instead of writing it on paper that could be circulated or read by anyone at the front desk.

Patients with balances due or large deductibles could also use the tablets to set up their own payment plans. This way, they could commit to modest monthly charges to their credit or debit card discreetly, avoiding the embarrassment of revealing they couldn't pay in full immediately. Patients would feel more comfortable, and the practice would get paid more reliably, with fewer costly mailings and collection calls.

Building on success

With patient behavior at the core of the practice's collection problems, technology could not correct all issues overnight. But it did allow the team to make a huge improvement in practice finances. And they were on their way to much better relationships with patients, even as they were collecting from them more reliably.

Putting better insurance information in schedulers' hands on-demand gave the team more confidence in discussing payment requirements with patients. Repeating the same message both when scheduling and via the tablet system at reception helped the practice gradually correct the gross misunderstanding many patients had about copayments being discretionary for the practice. As staff made payment terms clearer, patients complied with them more often.

Within a month of implementing the payment portal, eligibility checking, custom reminders, and the tablets, the practice tripled its patient collections. The wolf was pushed back from the door! Best of all, the team was more upbeat and more empowered. Interactions with patients were less stressful. The practice now had a solid foundation to build on to continue improving collections and profitability.

Looking ahead, the manager has plans for more technology deployments in the front office. As patients adjust to paying copays at every visit, the next challenge will be collecting deductibles. The manager's plan is to give patients up-to-date deductible information at scheduling and check-in with estimation software.

Modernizing access to the practice with online scheduling—a reputation-boosting convenience for the practice's high-end market—is also on the agenda.

Takeaways from the cases: tools every practice should consider

There are three broad areas of front office technology that Capko & Morgan recommends every practice explore. These tools can bring almost immediate benefits to your practice, without a lot of overhead or hassle:

Verification and estimation tools: These products include *real-time eligibility checking* (software that verifies coverage and retrieves basic terms in moments); *patient payment estimators* (software that calculates patient payment responsibility, based on most current data from the payer); and *electronic prior authorization, or ePA* (software that enables requesting and receiving prior authorization for medications and services via the internet).

Eligibility checking (aka insurance verification, or real-time insurance verification) has come so far, so fast that it is now commonly available as a standard PMS feature. Even if you haven't tried it yet, you may already have access to this invaluable timesaver. We've worked with numerous practices in which no one was aware that this tool existed, or how helpful it is—and PMS vendors have told us that they've also been surprised by how many of their clients are slow to take advantage of it.

Real-time eligibility checking can make the scheduling and check-in processes faster, but that's not the only way it improves front office performance. It also lessens the chance of unintentionally seeing a patient out of network. And because the eligibility reply is automatically captured in the patient's record, it reduces data entry.

Patient payment estimators are less commonly available as PMS features. An increasing number of excellent add-on solutions bundle insurance verification (helpful if your PMS doesn't offer it), credit card processing, and sometimes even secure credit-card-on-file service with estimation into one product. Some tablet and kiosk check-in systems also include estimation, credit card processing, and even secure credit-card-on-file solutions, so that patients can set up their own payment plans.

Electronic prior authorization (ePA) is a time-saving technology that has gained momentum in the past couple of years. Third-party ePA software (such as CoverMyMeds.com and Surescripts) enables requesting and receiving prior authorization for medications without faxing, phoning, or using a payer's (often complex) online form. Some practice management systems have partnered with ePA technology vendors to integrate their solutions, so that staff can request authorizations from within the patient's demographic record. But even when full integration isn't possible, using these systems as standalones can significantly reduce the burden of prior authorizations for practices that often need to request them.

Patient payment solutions: Solutions like payment portals, email statements, and credit-card-on-file systems all aim to address two huge trends affecting practices: the shifting of payment responsibility to patients, and consumers' increasing preference for paying electronically.

Patient payments now account for 25%-40% of collectable revenue for most practices that contract with health plans. To protect profitability, practices simply must master collecting from patients—and they must learn to do it while maintaining positive relationships.

The consumer trend favoring electronic payments can actually be a godsend to practice, if you embrace it. By allowing patients to pay the way they prefer, you'll be able to get paid faster and more reliably. Your patients will save time, paper, and postage, and your practice will, too. You'll be viewed more favorably by your patients[28], while also getting paid more reliably, and with lower collection cost. It's the epitome of a win-win.

Electronic payment options can take many forms at your practice. A straightforward way to start is to open a payment portal and start offering email statements, so that patients can click over to pay using whatever connected device they like. Like our case study client, you may find that your PMS offers a payment portal you can simply enable. But if not, there are third party options available.

For patients with large deductibles and pending surgery, maternity, or other significant expense, payment terms can be a welcome help. Customized, automatic deductions from a debit or credit card are easier for them and for your practice. But you must be able to do this in compliance with PCIDSS (payment card industry data security standards). Credit-card-on-file systems built into check-in tablets and payment estimation systems usually offer this protection.

Patient services and engagement: Along with the trend favoring online payments, people increasingly use their connected devices for booking services and receiving reminders. They're able to make purchases and book other types of services without picking up the phone, at times convenient for them—and they'd like to do so with healthcare, too. Practices that offer this convenience will get a leg up as gen x and millennial patients age and start using more healthcare services.

---

[28]Fiserv has done an excellent series of annual studies of consumer trends and attitudes related to payment channels. See: https://www.fiserv.com/resources/413-13-17891-COL_2.5_RP_SixthAnnualBHS-2013_HR_121013.pdf

Practices are often hesitant to offer online booking. Sometimes the concern is integration with their PMS and EHR—but as with insurance verification, you might find that your vendor has already created a built-in solution you can use. Even if not, third party solutions have evolved dramatically in the past few years. Many of the newest options offer integrated reputation management tools. These allow you to easily request feedback and reviews from patients who booked online. This is another win-win: you'll be able to easily encourage patients who just used a service they value (online scheduling) to help build your online reputation.

Most of these systems also offer automated reminders—another option greatly valued by connected patients. These don't have to replace phone reminders, if voice contact works better for some patients. Automated reminders can be like adding a belt to suspenders: an extra protection against no-shows. The cost is minimal, and the potential savings from avoided no-shows can be dramatic.

Some PMSs also offer waiting lists—another tool that can automate a time-consuming process and allow your practice to give more attentive service. Plus, being able to fill freed-up slots not only pleases patients by getting them in sooner, it helps maximize productivity (yet another win-win).

Be open to workflow adjustments

You may need to tweak your workflow to get the most benefit from new technologies. This may sound daunting, but refining your workflow at the same time you implement technology can free up staff time for more valuable tasks or enable staff to complete their work more quickly (or both). It's helpful to think of your practice workflow as a continuous improvement project—never perfect, never finished, always evolving to better support your practice's productivity.

For example, many practices have evolved elaborate work-arounds to try to prevent patients from unintentionally being seen out-of-network or being surprised at the front desk by a collection request. We've seen practices that involve the billing team during scheduling, during check-in, or both to try to be fully sure about eligibility and to present accurate payment information to patients.

These types of workflow contortions are born of desperation and necessity because practices have paid a steep price for unreliable insurance verification and failing to collect well from patients. Practices are often reluctant to let go of these procedures and their extra steps—even when technology can do the job better with a lot less effort. Take a close look at all the steps of your workflow. Carefully evaluating whether certain workarounds have become redundant can help you take full advantage of the opportunity to be more efficient.

It's also easy to become wedded to a certain order of doing things. But technology may make it more efficient to rethink the sequence. For example, as more patients book via online scheduling, you'll be able to collect email addresses in advance. That can enable your scheduling team to get patients set up with payment and even EHR portal accounts before they even arrive for their first visit. That, in turn, makes it easier for staff to ask patients to complete their patient information online before they arrive.

Schedulers' jobs can also evolve to include verifying and editing appointments that patients book themselves, not just taking inbound calls for appointments. Practices sometimes delay offering online appointment scheduling because they're worried about patients choosing inappropriate slots, but many practices have more types of slots than they actually need. Analyzing your visits over a test period can help you narrow down your slot times to just two or three, making the risk of a patient choosing incorrectly less of an issue. Schedulers can make checking and correcting patient appointments, plus managing waiting lists, part of their redefined role.

One of the best aspects of being open to changing workflow rules is the opportunity to add tasks that fell through the cracks or were put on the back burner. Managing waiting lists to get anxious patients in sooner is a task often left undone; paying more attention to them gives patients better service and helps maintain productivity. Patient recalls are another excellent opportunity that many practices just haven't had time to take on in an organized way. Having a system in place to proactively book follow-up visits or preventive care helps patients stay healthier, shows your practice cares, and also smooths out revenue.

Managing your practice's online reputation, both with physician ratings sites and with payer directories, is yet another important task that many practices don't find enough staff time for. As technology makes some tasks easier, schedulers and receptionists will have time to monitor and manage your practice's online profiles. And as technology helps speed up other tasks, staff can also spend a bit more time with patients. Checking in with them during their time at the practice, and asking their opinions before they leave, is a way everyone can contribute to polishing the practice's reputation without technology—and it can boost engagement, too.

Avoiding all-or-nothing thinking

When considering technology solutions, the perfect shouldn't be the enemy of the good. With all of the complexities of today's healthcare infrastructure, plus the spectrum of patient preferences, it's unlikely that any technology will work perfectly in every situation. But don't let that stop you from taking advantage of the benefits a solution can offer you and your patients.

With both estimation and real-time verification software, for example, you will likely find some of your plans won't communicate with the software, or will send only partial information. This can mean that some manual verification will still be part of your workflow. But even if as much as 20% of verification must be done the old way—visiting the plan's website, or even calling the plan—you'll gain a big advantage in accuracy and speed on 80% of your appointments. And the systems will continue to improve: Remember that health plans have nearly as much to gain as you do from streamlining these task.

Similarly, with online scheduling and both EHR and payment portals, not all patients will want to use them. But those that do will value them highly—and they will save staff considerable time.

Consider an example from another industry: automated teller machines (ATMs). It took a very long time for ATMs to become ubiquitous. When they first rolled out decades ago, most bank customers didn't use them. But the few that did tapped into a convenience they valued, while also saving their bank money. Over time, utilization grew, and now pretty much everyone uses an ATM at least occasionally. That hasn't eliminated the need for human tellers for some transactions—and that's okay. The bank and the consumer still win whenever the ATM can do the job faster and more conveniently.

Be real about ROI

It's easy to underestimate the value of a technology solution by looking only at direct costs. For example, when looking at a tablet or kiosk solution for your front desk, you'll likely have hardware and software costs. But some of these costs may be replacing other direct expenses, such as credit card processing fees that are similar to what you're already paying a (different) processor.

Be sure to consider other expenses that will be avoided in your analysis. If you're currently sending statements to bill for copays and deductible payments, for example, then solutions like check-in tablets and credit-card-on-file systems can significantly cut down on these mailings—and their costs. As payment compliance improves, you may also avoid bad debt.

All the technologies discussed in this part of the book also have the potential to make your practice more productive—meaning you could see more patients each day. Consider how many additional appointments you could complete each week, and how that potential revenue compares to the technology investment. Remember also to factor in how changing up your reminders and offering online scheduling could reduce no-shows and improve average productivity.

Consider all of these factors, being as quantitative as you can, when evaluating the positive impact of adding new technologies against the out-of-pocket costs:

- Bad debt reduction
- Paper and postage
- Labor (mailings, check deposits, collection calls)
- Time value of money (especially if you're frequently using credit)
- Capacity for additional visits
- Reduced revenue losses from no-shows

Don't do it all yourself

Practices miss out on new features from their EHR and PMS vendors because frequent updates slip through unnoticed. And why is that? Because managers and physician owners are far too busy to read every message from eager vendors!

You can solve this problem by appointing tech-savvy staff as liaisons to your key vendors. You'll be less likely to miss out on important updates and promising third-party add-ons in the future. And you'll provide growth and job variety for motivated employees.

Above all, give things a try

The annoyances of legacy infrastructure and the burdens regulation places on technology can make it seem like an expensive pain-in-the-neck that's bound to disappoint. But there actually are technology innovations happening that are driven primarily by your needs. They're not all perfect: Even when developers focus on your needs, they will still sometimes fall short. But many of these newer products are easy to try, and priced with consideration for your ROI.

With your whole team engaged in monitoring technology innovation, it will be much easier to learn about new options and give them a try. So do it! Remember that the downside risk is often a lot smaller than you might think, and the upside for your practice can be significant.

INDEX

Made in the USA
Monee, IL
13 June 2022

97932329R00116